All Things
REAL ESTATE ^{SM}

®

Selling · Buying · Renting

FIFTH EDITION

Written by the nation's leading residential real estate expert whose companies handled the sale, purchase, mortgage financing and rental of over 250,000 homes in all 50 states

Walter Hall

Auctoris
Press 📖

NORWELL, MASSACHUSETTS

Auctoris
Press 🕮

Auctoris Press
P.O. Box 274
Norwell, MA 02061

All Things REAL ESTATE by Walter Hall
www.allthingsrealestate.org

ISBN 978-0-9778023-6-4
LCCN 2015909328

Publisher's Cataloging-In-Publication Data
(Prepared by The Donohue Group, Inc.)

Hall, Walter R., Jr.
   All Things REAL ESTATE : selling-buying-renting / Walter Hall.

      pages ; cm

   Includes index.
   "A guide for homeowners, home sellers and buyers, landlords, tenants
and real estate agents who are searching for a practical, proven solution to
their most pressing real estate questions and concerns. Written by the nation's
leading residential real estate expert."
   Issued also as an ebook.
   ISBN: 978-0-9778023-6-4

   1. Real estate business--United States--Handbooks, manuals, etc.
2. Residential real estate--United States--Handbooks, manuals, etc. I. Title.
II. Title: Real estate

HD1381.5.U55 H35 2015
333.330973

Cover by McConnell Design, info@mcconnelldesign.com
Interior layout and design by KnockoutDesign, www.knockoutbooks.com

Printed in the United States of America

CONTENTS

PART III Home Sellers & Buyers   57

PART IV Cyclical Market Issues   65

PART V Landlords   71

Introduction

Buying or Selling —
WHAT YOU NEED TO KNOW

Most of this book is devoted to home sellers and buyers. However, the concepts and principles described apply as well to commercial and industrial real estate, as well as tenants and landlords. So, for those of you in this category, merely substitute "tenant" for "buyer"—"landlord" for "seller"—and "rental" for "home."

Timing is (Almost) Everything

Historically, each real estate boom has ultimately become a bust to some degree. What goes up in real estate usually goes down. The degree of "down" almost always depends on the intensity and corresponding speed of price increase on the "up" side. Generally, if the up side is gradual, the down side will be slight or mild. However, if that up side was fast and intense with big, rapid price increases, the odds are that the down side will likely mirror it.

So it's safe to say that the real estate market is dynamic, constantly changing—directly impacting home buyers and sellers in four major ways:

- Home values and trends
- Marketing time (for sellers to sell their home)
- Cost of sale (a seller's marketing cost)
- Who has the negotiation advantage: seller, buyer, neither?

Defining the Market

The very best way to determine the current real estate market and trend in a specific metropolitan area, community (ZIP code),

7

neighborhood or price range, is to know the current supply (and prior 3–6 month trend) of unsold home listings in these different geographic areas and price range groupings. "Supply" is expressed by the number of months it would take to sell the current inventory of unsold homes at the current rate of home sales. For example, assume 1,200 unsold homes at the end of the month, with 200 sales taking place the same month. Therefore, there is a six month supply of unsold homes, based on the current rate of sales. (1,200 divided by 200).

Real estate professionals have long held that a six month supply is indicative of what is referred to as a "Balanced Market"—the number of sellers and buyers about equal with home values holding steady. Other indications of a Balanced Market are normal home marketing time (60–90 days), normal seller's cost of sale, and neither seller nor buyer having a negotiation advantage. Major negotiations involve price and the key terms of sale, such as the amount of deposit, mortgage and property inspection contingencies, and time to close (transfer title).

Five Market Conditions

There are five distinct market conditions with corresponding impact to buyers and sellers:

Intense Sellers' Market — (less than four month supply of unsold home listings)
Many more buyers than sellers: home values rapidly increasing, marketing time greatly reduced, lowest sale cost, negotiations strongly favoring sellers.

Moderate Sellers' Market — (4.1 to 5.9 month supply)
Slightly more buyers than sellers: home values slightly increasing, marketing time slightly reduced, lower sale cost, negotiations slightly favoring sellers.

Balanced Market — (6 to 6.9 month supply)
Equal number of buyers and sellers: home values holding, normal marketing time, normal sale cost, negotiations favoring neither seller nor buyer.

Moderate Buyers' Market — (7 to 8.9 month supply)
Slightly more sellers than buyers: home values slightly decreasing, marketing time slightly increased, higher sale cost, negotiations slightly favoring buyers.

Intense Buyers' Market — (over 9 month supply)
Many more sellers than buyers: home values rapidly decreasing, marketing time greatly increased, highest sale cost, negotiations strongly favoring buyers.

It's important to point out that any broad (or macro) market area—such as a suburban area or county, or even a specific community—can contain a number of micro markets made up of specific neighborhoods and/or price ranges. These micro-markets can differ greatly from the macro markets in which they exist. For example, a whole community could be defined as currently experiencing an "Intense Buyers' Market"—but a certain price range in certain neighborhoods could simultaneously be experiencing a "Moderate Sellers' Market."

Where To Get The Data

For home buyers interested in buying a home in a specific community (ZIP code), this data is usually easily available by real estate agents through their local Multiple Listing Service (MLS). As stated above, broad community data should be viewed as a macro market which provides a general feel for the overall community—not the specific price range or part of town in which a buyer may be interested. Most MLS systems can also provide data on unsold home inventory in a specific community and price range, which will give buyers a very

9

clear picture of the type of market they're buying into—and therefore, the advantages or disadvantages they will face.

For home sellers looking to set a competitive price on their home, this exercise is simplified, as a seller's property can be matched (by MLS data) to recently sold and currently unsold similar homes in the same community or similar nearby communities.

Homes Don't Exist in a Vacuum

For home sellers, the single, most important thing to understand is that their home is going to be compared to other homes for sale that are similar in price range and location. That location may not only be in the town (or city) their home is located in, but a specific, similar neighborhood in an adjacent or nearby town. Studies by the National Association of Realtors document that the typical buyer looks at no less than 10 homes for sale before making the final decision to buy one. If a seller's home does not compete with the price, condition, quality and location of those homes competing for buyers, that home will not sell.

For home buyers, the single, most important thing to understand is the market conditions that exist in the price range and locations they are interested in. See *Five Market Conditions* on page 8.

Urban, Suburban and Rural Data

There are many references in this book about the MLS (Multiple Listing Service) and the use of the home data contained therein that is very useful to both sellers and buyers. Most urban and suburban markets have an MLS. However, chances are that an MLS-type system is not available in rural areas. Therefore, the real estate agent will have to manually gather the necessary data needed to advise clients properly.

— WALTER HALL, Norwell, Massachusetts

PART I

Home Sellers
and
Homeowners

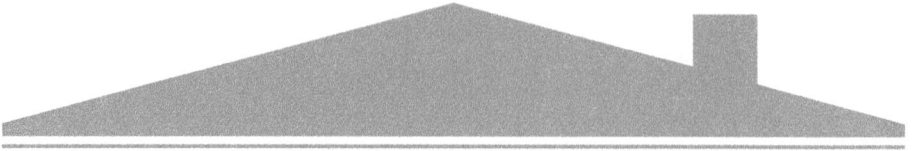

(1) PRICING YOUR HOME

This is the most important and toughest decision you will have to make: setting the initial list price. Take your time and consider all of the following before making this key decision.

First Offer = Best Offer

What most home sellers don't appreciate is that the very best opportunity to get the highest possible price is in the very early stages of marketing their home. Here's why: according to a survey by the National Association of Realtors, the average buyer searched for seven weeks and inspected ten homes before finding the home they ultimately purchased. Consider this: if there were 10 new buyers entering the market each week looking for homes in your price range and community, then the day your home went on the market, there would be a pool of 70 potential buyers who would consider your home. Lots of competition for *fresh merchandise*. You get one shot at this pool, and this is invariably the best time to get the highest possible price for the least marketing time, effort and cost. And that's also why your first offer will probably be your best offer.

Getting the Price Right

However, you won't get that "highest possible price" if you've overpriced your home during this critical, initial phase. Potential buyers won't even look at it. So, how do you avoid pricing your home out of the market? Estimating the probable sale price of a home is not complex; proven approaches to estimating value have been around for a long time. Real estate professionals will study the prices of recently sold properties and current listings similar to yours in terms of size, features, condition, and neighborhood. Next, dollar adjustments will be made, up or down, for major differences (between your home and each similar home recently sold) including number of rooms, square footage, overall condition, lot size, and more. From this research and analysis a "Range of Value" can be established. Your home will most likely sell for a price within this Range of Value, and your initial list price should be just under the high end of the Range. Your final sale price, whether at the top, middle, or bottom of the Range of Value, will be influenced mostly by your initial list price. For detailed information on estimating a sale price, see *A True Story* on page 17 and *Exhibit A1* on page 89.

Buyers Buy By Comparison

Today, people shop (make comparisons) in order to be assured of value. They compare values in appliances, automobiles and a host of other commodities. Homes are no exception; they also are purchased on a comparative basis, as to location, size, condition, amenities and, above all, price.

Consider Market Conditions

In markets that are experiencing recent reductions in home values, there is another important dimension to take into consideration. The normal conveyance period—the time from agreeing to buy a home to the time it closes (title is transferred)—is in the range of 60–90 days. Sale prices are not recorded and documented for the public record until the closing. Therefore, in a market that's experiencing a reduction in home values, what you see as a recorded purchase price today, was really the market price 60–90 earlier. Much could have changed in the interim that might cause a buyer to either not buy or pay less today than 60–90 days earlier. Point? If all indications are that the market is trending to a Buyers' Market—as indicated by fewer sales and more listings in the recent past—you should definitely discount the documented sale prices you see for similar homes when comparing these homes to the value of your home.

Consider Competing Homes

You should also study similar homes/locations that are currently competing with your home for buyers, so you can get an even better feel for the current market. How long have these similar homes been on the market? What was their initial list price? What's their current list price? How many similar homes are out there currently competing with your home for buyers? How many one, three and six months ago? What's the trend as it impacts the price and sale of your home?

Consider Gen X/Y Buyers (Millennials)

More and more buyers fall into this age group, so it's important for you to understand their familiarity and reliance on the Internet to research things of interest or importance to them. You can rest assured that buying a house certainly falls into this category. The point is that you can be certain that if they are interested in your home they will have researched all the approaches to value described above, and will be able to back up their offer price with documented facts.

Consider Local "Price Ranges"

One last point on pricing your home: be very aware of price *ranges*. Generally, buyers look at homes within certain price ranges or *caps*. If you learn that the value of your home is at or somewhere near the cusp between two distinct ranges, it's always best to be, at most, at the very top of the lower range.

② MAXIMIZING YOUR EQUITY

With the big dollars involved in real estate today, many home sellers lose sight of the fact that maximizing the equity in their home is simply the result of two things: getting the highest possible price and paying the least cost in doing so.

Getting the highest price possible relates specifically to setting a competitive, supportable list price at inception. If a home is priced within its documented Range of Value, the odds are very high it will sell quickly at the high end of the Range. If priced above the high end of the Range, the odds are very high it will take a long time to sell and when it eventually does, the price will be at or below the low end of the Range. For more details see *1–Pricing Your Home,* page 12.

3 MARKETING YOUR HOME

When selling a home, the seller's objective is to attract a qualified buyer ready, willing and able to buy at the highest possible price. The key to achieving these objectives is establishing a competitive, supportable list price from day one.

According to a survey by the National Association of Realtors, over 60% of buyers first learn about the home they ultimately buy from sources other than a real estate agent. The number one source today—and growing every day—is the Internet, followed by "For Sale" signs, and learning about the home from friends, relatives and neighbors. As sources of buyers, newspaper advertising and open houses run a distant fourth and fifth.

With that in mind, what follows are the major, most successful marketing strategies in play today, which are designed to maximize your home's exposure to the greatest number of potential buyers for the least cost. According to another survey by the National Association of Realtors, the average buyer searched for seven weeks and inspected ten homes before finding the home they ultimately purchased. During that time, they are actively searching out every home for sale in their price range and communities of their choice. If your home is priced too high (above its indicated Range of Value), most buyers will pass it by; if within the Range, they'll take a look. The more who look, the more likelihood of a buyer.

Internet Listings

With the majority of all home buyers starting their home search online (this number constantly increases) your home needs to be listed on the Internet in as many places as possible, including Realtor.com, Google, Zillow, Trulia, Homes.com and many more. And don't forget the social media. Listing your home in the local MLS starts the process.

MLS (Multiple Listing Service)

When your home is listed in the local area MLS, it is immediately exposed to thousands of its Realtor members and their agents giving you the broadest possible exposure to those buyers working with these agents. For details, see *27–What is MLS?* on page 59. All MLS listings are linked to Realtor.com, the most viewed real estate website.

Yard Sign

Having a distinctive, professional looking yard sign in front of your home increases your chances of attracting *drive by* shoppers.

E-Mail Marketing

One of the simplest and most cost-effective tools for letting people know that you're selling your home is via e-mail. I'm not suggesting *spamming* your friends and relatives, but I do suggest sending a simple note to your neighbors and the people in your address book that says "We're Selling Our House." This can prove extremely effective. As these are people you know, they will likely be willing to pass your information along to their contacts. Before long, your message can reach hundreds of people—some of whom will very likely be in the market for a home. Best of all, it's done at no cost to you.

A short, simple note that includes a link to your home's listing on the Internet is all you need. Encourage them to check it out, and let them know that they can feel free to pass your information along to others. The following sample e-mail message can be used or edited as you see fit.

Hello, Friends:

We are selling our home at 1003 Main Street in Belmont, and would be most appreciative if you could pass this information along to anyone you know who might be interested.

Photos of our home can be accessed via this link: 12w3k33w. com. Interested parties can also call our listing agent, John Price, at 781-555-1234 for more information or to schedule a showing. Thank you for your help!

Dick & Jan

And don't forget the entire scope of social media to promote the sale of your home, including Facebook, YouTube, Twitter, and more.

A True Story:
Using Technology to Sell Your Home—*For the Highest Price*

In today's real estate market, the smart way to sell your home for top dollar is to utilize the most modern data and technology available to research and evaluate all the major factors bearing on pricing and selling your home for the highest *supportable* price. I emphasize "supportable" because today's typical buyer has used the same modern data and technology to research and evaluate what would constitute a fair and competitive purchase price for your home.

MLS Data

As a *real world* example, I will explain how I helped a client accomplish that objective. Bob and Sally had a home that they estimated was "worth at least $500,000." My first step was to gain access to MLS data on thousands of homes for sale and sold, zeroing in on Bob and Sally's community and neighborhood market and those in the area that competed for buyers in the same type of market.

Property Inspection

My next step was to inspect their property, listing all the relevant data such as location, size (square feet of living space), land area, and more. With that data in hand, I gathered recent sales data on similar homes, in a similar broad price range ($450,000–$550,000) and in the same community as Bob and Sally's home, as well as similar neighborhoods in communities that competed for buyers with Bob and Sally's community and price range.

The Art of Appraising (Estimating) Home Value

Buyers buy by comparison—whether for cars, appliances, or just about everything else. Homes are no exception. In advising Bob and Sally on setting a competitive, supportable listing price, my research essentially focused on the sale price of recently sold similar homes in similar locations, and the same price range. Once I had gathered data on four homes that met that criteria, I compared each one to Bob and Sally's and made plus and minus adjustments to their actual sale price to reflect amenities and conditions that were more or less favorable than Bob and Sally's home. See *Exhibit A1, Home Appraisal Format* on page 89.

As an example of an *adjustment*, assume the following: one of the similar homes—which sold for $420,000—was identical to Bob and Sally's except it had a two-car garage, but Bob and Sally's had a three car garage. At that time, an extra one-car garage space would cost close to $2,500, so Bob and Sally got an estimated value of $422,500 when compared to this similar home. I went through the same exercise on the other three similar homes, resulting in a variety of plus and minus adjustments to Bob and Sally's home.

Evaluating Similar Homes Still For Sale

As to similar homes in similar locations that were still for sale, the only value they have for research and analysis is how long they have been on the market, what their starting price was, and what the current price is. This gives some indication as to pricing that hasn't produced a buyer, as well as potential competition to attract buyers if and when their pricing reflects reality.

Range of Value

My research clearly showed that the current market indicated that the Range of Value of Bob and Sally's home was $425,000 to $450,000, with a probable final sale price somewhere in the middle.

I presented my findings and strongly recommended that they initially list their home for $449,000, leaving themselves some bargaining room. If they had told me that they still felt their home was worth more than that and they would put it on the market above my recommended price to see if they could "get our price," I would further advise them that in my experience, this almost never happens. Today, buyers are just too smart and have done their own research. But they didn't tell me that, because they were highly motivated to sell.

A Happy Ending

Here's the end of the story: they listed their home for $449,000 and got four offers the first two weeks, ranging from $427,000 to $439,000, and ultimately the party making the low offer finally upped it to $442,000. A happy ending—the best kind.

Real Estate Broker or Do It Yourself?

No description of marketing your home would be complete without a few comments on this subject. You probably have a good idea of what the typical real estate firm offers in the way of services. If you're not sure, see **26–About Real Estate Commissions** on page 59.

As to trying to do it yourself, this is not for everyone and it is not recommended for any home seller needing to sell in a buyers' market. Conversely, if you do try to sell your home on your own, the best time to try this is in a sellers' market—preferably an intense sellers' market. When weighing the pros and cons of selling your home on your own, carefully consider the services and activities most often required by home sellers and/or their real estate and legal representatives. Each one takes time. Most require expertise as well. All cost money.

Finding the Buyer

Experience proves that in order to maximize the likelihood of attracting a buyer and achieving the highest price possible, all marketing channels should be employed, including listing on key web sites, an attractive "For Sale" sign, an offering brochure, e-mail marketing, direct mail campaigns, and availability to schedule and handle appointments to show your home to prospective buyers.

Making the Sale

Being prepared in advance to decisively close the qualified buyer—from both a price and legal protection standpoint—often makes the difference between a clean sale at top dollar versus a muddled transaction that might or might not close at a less than desired price. An Offer Form and/or Purchase & Sale Agreement have to be prepared.

Keeping the Sale Together

Most real estate and legal practitioners know that much can transpire between the time of the agreement to sell and the transfer of title that can kill the transaction or put it in serious jeopardy if not attended to in a timely and professional manner.

Closing the Sale

With the increasing trend of post-closing litigation, the need for home sellers to have specialized real estate legal representation, prior to and at the closing, is becoming increasingly important.

(4) OPEN HOUSES

While open houses can be considered a tool for marketing your home, it can be difficult to discern true buyers from people who are simply out for a Sunday drive or trolling for new interior design ideas.

In my experience, pre-scheduled showings—where a buyer has specifically come forward to request an appointment to see your home—is the ideal, but is not as effective in producing buyer foot traffic as open houses. As to scheduling more than one open house, I recommend additional ones be held only concurrent with price breaks.

That said, if you do decide to conduct an open house, here are my recommendations:

- The best time for an open house is traditionally Sunday between noon and 4:00 PM, lasting no longer than two hours.
- Place an open house sign in front of your property and directional signs at the end of your street.
- Have an *Information Packet* available for interested buyers containing such things as a copy of your deed, plot plan, and details of normal property-related expenses such as taxes, cost of electricity, and more.
- Be sure to "stage" your home properly. For details, see *5–Staging Your Home* on page 22.

- Refreshments are a nice touch and promote a welcoming atmosphere.

- Allow buyers to roam freely about your home—don't shadow them or make them feel uncomfortable.

- Be sure to mention special features of your home that may not be obvious.

- Because you've opened your door to anyone off the street, best to remove valuable objects from your home and store them in a safe place. Although most people are honest, it is better to be safe and take precautions rather than be sorry later on.

5 STAGING YOUR HOME TO SELL

It's vital that you create the best first impression possible when your home is on the market. An important point to remember is that you actually have to sell your home three times: (1) to the buyer; (2) to the home inspector; and (3) to the mortgage lender's appraiser. It's a fact that in most cases, homes will sell more easily if they are furnished and occupied. There's just no substitute for that warm, lived-in feeling when selling a home. Many buyers have difficulty visualizing what a vacant home will look like when furnished. That is why many builders furnish a model home.

When evaluating the condition of your home, always think of it from the buyer's point of view, not yours. Real estate professionals know, from long experience, that it's not usually one little thing that turns off prospective buyers. It's most often an accumulation of many little things that add up to a low offer or a lost sale.

The importance of preparing, or staging, your home when you are selling cannot be emphasized enough. The goal is simple but important—help buyers see *everything* your house and grounds have to offer, and take the focus away from your personal items. The following lists will give you ideas, how-to's, and perspectives to ensure that your home shows well inside and out. When you stage your home, you should be packing many of your belongings that you don't need on a daily basis. This will greatly increase the feeling of space in your home, and since many people move because they need more space, it's win-win for everyone.

When your house is staged, it is also ready to be photographed; good photos make a good first impression when buyers see your property during an Internet search, and they increase the likelihood that a showing will be scheduled. Here are some **Staging Tips:**

Outside

Does your property have what the pros call *curb appeal*? Upon driving up to your home, will the buyer want to take a look inside? Here are some tips to avoid the turn-offs:

- Water and mow the lawn regularly and patch any bare spots in the lawn.
- Trim shrubs to below window sill height, if appropriate.
- Plant some flowers, especially near the front door.
- Touch-up or re-paint as necessary for best appearance.
- Sweep the driveway and sidewalks on a regular basis.
- Apply mulch around shrubs and trees for a neat appearance and keep weeds pulled.
- Clean out the gutters and downspouts.
- Make sure trash barrels are hidden from view.

Inside

First things first: if the entrance into your home is dark, consider repainting it using a light color. Also, make sure it is well lit with warm lights. Your living/family room and kitchen are the two most important rooms in your home to a buyer. Here is where they will most likely be spending most of their waking hours. They will be very carefully inspected, as will the bathrooms. Some helpful tips to show the interior of your home to its best advantage:

- Make certain your home is free of offensive odors. Tobacco smoke and pet-related odors are equally offensive and will turn buyers off.

- Beds should always be made.

- Patch cracked plaster, fix loose doorknobs and crooked light fixtures.

- If you decide to repaint, use lighter/brighter colors to give the illusion of space.

- Make sure your cellar and garage are neat and well organized.

- De-clutter!!! At this time your house should be decorated to show off the best features of the house, not your stuff. Buyers are not buying your stuff; they are buying the house.

- Remove extra side chairs, side tables, trunks, and anything else that is touching the floor that isn't absolutely necessary for the next few months. This is a no-cost way to increase the apparent square footage of the house.

- If your dining room has always felt too small due to a large china cabinet or sideboard (or both), remove them.

- Clean the house from top to bottom, then keep it clean. Wash the windows and have the carpets professionally cleaned.

- Make sure all lamps and light fixtures have the highest wattage bulbs acceptable and that all fixtures, lamps, and light switches are in working order. Turn on the lights before prospective buyers arrive for a tour.

- Organize the kitchen cabinets so they appear spacious. Clear off the counters of all but 1 or 2 small appliances.

- Pack away seasonal clothing from all closets to increase the appearance of space. Ditto for any other items in your closets that aren't absolutely needed. Try to clear the closet floor—it'll make the closet look bigger.

- Complete the little repairs that you've been meaning to accomplish.

- If the carpeting is in poor condition or if it has pet stains or odors, replace it with new carpet in a neutral color.

- Bathrooms should be spotless and mildew-free. Replace any lighting or plumbing fixtures that have corrosion damage. Replace mildewed caulk in the tub/shower.

- If appropriate, rent a storage locker to store all your extra stuff.

Basement/Attic/Garage/Shed

- Throw away all the old clothes, toys, broken appliances, scrap pieces of wood, empty boxes, etcetera that have been accumulating. Pack up the items you are keeping in well labeled boxes, then vacuum thoroughly. Many people dislike basement and attic spaces and they'll feel better about yours if it is clean and orderly.

- Try to clean out the garage so you can get the cars in; if the cars are in the garage, it will give the impression that there is plenty of storage space in the house.

- If at all possible, store boats or RVs off-site.

All in all, you need to make sure that the exterior and interior of your home is in the best possible condition.

6 SHOWING YOUR HOME

Getting Your Home Ready for Showings

Showing your home is a pivotal point in the selling process, so it's vital that you prepare, or stage, your home to create the best first impression possible. When evaluating the condition of your home, always think of it from the buyer's point of view, not yours.

Showing Your Home

Showing your home to prospective buyers and/or their agent is relatively simple—here are a few things to keep in mind:

- If you happen to be home during a showing, allow the agent and buyers to roam freely about the home; don't shadow them or make them feel uncomfortable.

- Be certain to mention any special features of your home that might not be obvious.

- If the agent or the buyers ask you a question, answer it completely and honestly; withholding information can have a very negative impact further along in the process.

- Have a binder prepared in advance that has your current annual real estate taxes and cost of (if applicable) heating, electricity, gas, water and sewerage bills. Most buyers are interested in these costs.

- Make sure the binder is well labeled and located in an obvious place so agents and buyers can review it if you are not home during the showing.

- Interested buyers will want a clear understanding of the boundaries of your lot; therefore, it could be beneficial to have a copy of your deed and plot plan (if you have one) in the binder as well.

- Remove valuable objects from your home and store them in a safe location. Although most people are honest and don't go around stealing or breaking things, it is better to be safe and take appropriate precautions.

⑦ YOUR SALE DOCUMENTS

NOTE: *what follows reflects the practices and nomenclature used in most East Coast states. Although practices and nomenclature vary throughout the rest of the country, the basic concepts apply universally.*

There are two primary sale documents involved in real estate transactions today:

Offer to Purchase — Essentially, the Offer to Purchase document is used to identify certain major issues, including: Purchase Price, How Payable, Duration of the Offer, Agreement to complete a full Purchase & Sale (P&S) Agreement within a certain time frame, and setting deadlines for the buyer to complete a property inspection and secure a firm mortgage commitment. Also, the conveyance period (days from accepted offer to closing) is specified. See *Exhibit B1* on page 108.

Purchase & Sale (P&S) Agreement — The P&S Agreement is a legally binding contract that reaffirms the Offer to Purchase and sets forth all the terms and conditions of the transaction. A typical P&S addresses at least 29 separate subjects. It is advisable to have a real estate attorney review the P&S Agreement to ensure that your interests in the transaction are properly represented and respected. Real estate professionals are prohibited from offering legal advice or opinion. See *Exhibit A2* on page 91.

Other Considerations

Earnest Money Deposit — Normally, a relatively small portion of the deposit (say $1,000) accompanies the Offer to Purchase form which specifies that this initial deposit will be added to, if and when the offer is accepted and a formal P&S is signed by both parties. Once this takes place, a total earnest money deposit of 5% (of the purchase price) is recommended. In any event, the earnest money deposit should be sufficient for the buyer to think twice about forfeiting the deposit if he/she decides to walk away from the transaction. However, this is one term of sale that is particularly sensitive to market conditions. If a Sellers' Market, you can usually hold out for a high earnest money deposit. In this case, you, the seller, are negotiating from a position of strength (*plenty of buyers out there*). Conversely, you may meet strong opposition to a high earnest money deposit if you find yourself in a Buyers' Market. Be that as it may, you should always strive for a *sufficient* earnest money deposit. The more *sufficient* the more *earnest.*

All deposits from the buyer should be placed in an escrow account with the listing broker, escrow company, or the seller's attorney, and these funds should remain in escrow until the closing. In the event that the closing does not occur, the funds cannot be released until both parties have agreed to the disposition of the funds in accordance with the terms and conditions set forth in the P&S.

Normal Contingencies

- **The mortgage contingency** makes the sale subject to the buyer getting a firm mortgage commitment for no less than a specified amount. This usually takes two to three weeks.

- **The home inspection contingency** provides the buyer a period of opportunity to hire a property inspection company to inspect the property. The home inspection contingency is usually completed within 10 days from acceptance of the offer by both parties. Issues should be addressed and, if necessary, resolved and incorporated in the P&S Agreement.

Disclosure — Make absolutely sure you haven't unintentionally misrepresented or failed to disclose known defects regarding any aspect of the condition of your property: structural, electrical, plumbing, drainage, heating, and air conditioning. When you sign the formal Purchase & Sale Agreement, it is strongly recommended that you provide the buyer a "Seller's Statement of Property Condition," disclosing in writing everything you know about the condition of your property that could potentially cause present or future problems for your buyer. The courts have repeatedly held that home sellers have the duty to disclose all known defects in the condition of their property, and can be held liable for failure to do so—not only pertaining to the buyer they sold to, but even subsequent buyers as well. See *Exhibit A3* on page 97 as well as *8–Disclosure Issues* below.

⑧ DISCLOSURE ISSUES

When you sell your home, the courts have held that you have a duty to disclose to the buyers <u>any and all</u> defects in the condition of the property known to you *or that should have been known by you.* Failure to disclose these defects can come back to haunt you years later at a very substantial cost in the form of both legal fees and payment for damages.

The usual components of the property that relate to disclosure are: **House Systems and Structures** (electric wiring, central air conditioning, plumbing), **Heating Systems, Insulation, Asbestos, Lead Paint, Land/Foundation** (earth instability, water/dampness in cellar), **Roof** (leaks, repairs), **Sewerage Private Systems** (backup, drainage problems), **Drainage/Water** (drainage, flooding problems), **Electrical Systems** (changes, repairs), **Neighborhood** (things like unusual noises), **Radon Gas/Mold.**

Make absolutely sure you haven't unintentionally misrepresented or failed to disclose known defects regarding any aspect of the condition of your property. When you sign the formal Purchase & Sale Agreement, it is strongly recommended that you provide the buyer a *Seller's Statement of Property Condition,* disclosing in writing everything you know about the condition of your property that could potentially cause present or future problems for your buyer—or subsequent buyers. See *Exhibit A3* on page 97.

⑨ KEEPING THE SALE TOGETHER

Many home sellers don't realize that there still remains much to do after the Purchase & Sale Agreement (P&S) has been signed. In fact, most real estate and legal practitioners know that much can transpire between the date of the P&S and the transfer of title that can kill the transaction or put it in serious jeopardy if not attended to in a timely and professional manner.

In this phase of the real estate transaction cycle, the seller's objective is to have no dilution of the price and terms agreed to in the P&S. One must ensure that all terms of the P&S are being met, including deadlines for property inspection and a firm mortgage commitment. Additionally, all last minute negotiations must be addressed and resolved, and a firm date and time for the closing must be scheduled. Lastly is the need for coordination of all the interested parties: lender's appraisers, home inspection company, engineers, and lender's attorney or escrow company.

⑩ GETTING READY FOR YOUR CLOSING

NOTE: What follows describes procedures and nomenclature throughout most of the East Coast. In other areas of the country these procedures generally take place, although some of the nomenclature may differ.

When your property is under agreement, you need to start preparing immediately for the closing. There is much for you to do between the sale date and the closing date in order to expedite the transaction and prevent delays and/or extra cost to you.

The Closing — If the buyer is obtaining a mortgage, the closing may be held at the office of the closing attorney representing the buyer's lender or, in many states, at the escrow company. You will be notified of the attorney's or closer's name and address, and will want to be informed by this individual of all issues that may require your involvement leading up to the closing.

Mortgage(s) — If your property is mortgaged, the lender(s) will have to be paid off at the time of closing. The closing attorney who usually represents the buyer's lender or the escrow company's closer will provide you with a written Mortgage Payoff Request Authorization, which allows the individual handling the closing to get exact payoff figures from your lender(s). You'll need to provide the name, address and telephone of your lender(s) and the account numbers. If one of your lenders has provided you with an Equity Credit Line, you will also have to provide the closer—before the closing—with a letter from that lender indicating that the credit line is frozen and specifying the outstanding balance. After your mortgage(s) have been paid in full, the lender(s) will send the closer a mortgage discharge document which the closer will then record at the municipal office where deeds are recorded.

The Deed — The preparation of a new deed to convey the property to the buyer is your responsibility. If you have an attorney representing you, you should advise the closer of the name and telephone number of the party preparing the deed. If you will not be represented by an attorney, the closer can prepare the deed at a reasonable cost.

Fire Department Certificates Needed (in most states)

- ▪ *Smoke Detector Certificate* — In accordance with most state's General Laws, you must obtain a Certificate of Compliance from your local fire department and bring it with you to the closing.

- ▪ *Carbon Monoxide Detector Certificate* — Most states require carbon monoxide detectors in any residence that contains fossil-fuel burning equipment (furnace, boiler, water heater, fireplace, or other device), or that has an attached garage. As with the smoke detector requirement, these laws and/or regulations are usually enforced by the local fire department during its inspection prior to the sale or transfer of your property.

Utilities Adjustments — A couple of weeks prior to the closing, you should contact all the utility companies to inform them of your move and to schedule final meter readings; this will also allow the buyers to begin setting up their accounts for the property.

Usually, the water, sewerage and heating oil adjustments are pro-rated on the anticipated day of occupancy; that is, after you have fully vacated and when the buyer moves in. If this date is going to coincide with the closing date (or very near that date) you can request that the closer handle the dollar adjustments on the **Closing Disclosure (Seller-Buyer)** (see *Exhibit A4* on page 99) by getting final readings and providing them to the closer no later than a few days before the closing. You must also advise all the utilities of the new owner as of the closing date (or occupancy date—whichever is earlier) and ask that your name be removed for billing purposes. If final readings cannot be provided to the closing attorney prior to the closing, they will have to be settled between you and the buyer independently.

Your Closing Costs — As the seller, in certain states you may be required to pay a *Conveyance Tax*. Other seller deductions include the selling broker commission if your home was sold by a broker, your portion of pro-rated taxes and assessments, recording fees, and legal fees if an attorney or escrow company is representing you. All of these costs are normally deducted from the proceeds of sale due you. Your net proceeds of sale will not be released to you until the deed and mortgage have been recorded. Most closing attorneys or escrow companies will make every effort to record documents and disburse the funds to you on the same day as the closing. All the dollars and cents involved in the transaction—as impacting both seller and buyer—are clearly documented in the **Closing Disclosure (Seller-Buyer)**—a copy of which may be found in *Exhibit A4* on page 99.

Condominiums — If you are selling a condominium unit, pursuant to the laws of most states, you are required to provide a certificate that lists the unpaid common expenses which have been assessed to your unit. This certificate can be obtained from your Condo Association. You will also be required to provide a Certificate of Insurance naming, as insured parties, *the buyer and the buyer's lender and its* *successors and assigns as their interest may appear*. This specific language must be on the Certificate of Insurance. See *11–If You Are Selling a Condominium* on page 34.

What To Bring To The Closing

▪ A final reading of your utilities, if appropriate (see above)

▪ A valid driver's license or other government issued identification

▪ Your Social Security Number(s). Federal law requires the closing attorney or escrow company to report the proceeds of the transaction to the IRS

▪ Your house keys, garage door openers, and any other applicable items

▪ All receipts and/or evidence of completed repairs (if required by the buyers)

▪ Your mortgage information (see above)

And Please Remember...

▪ Buyers usually request a final walk-through of your home within 24 hours prior to closing.

▪ Unless prior arrangements have been made with the buyers, your belongings should be moved out of the house prior to closing and the house should be "broom clean" (this is usually specified in the P&S). The buyers will have the expectation that they can begin to move in as soon as the deed is recorded.

▪ Before going to the closing, ALWAYS call the closing attorney or escrow company to verify that the closing is still on schedule.

▪ ALL parties named on the Deed must be present at the closing (with proof of identification) unless other arrangements, such as granting Power of Attorney, have been made and the closer has been made aware of these arrangements.

▪ To prepare a **Before Moving Check List** <u>and</u> **Moving Into Your New Home Check List**—see *Exhibit A5* on page 105.

11 IF YOU ARE SELLING A CONDOMINIUM

If you are selling a condominium, in most states you will be required to provide the following prior to closing:

Disclosure Certificate — This certificate can be obtained from your condominium association or property management company, and states that there are no unpaid condominium fees, special assessments, or other charges relating to your unit. You will need to provide the name of the buyer for this certificate so you will want to order it once you have secured a buyer. The certificate should have a date that coincides with the date of your closing. Condominium associations or property management companies often charge a fee for the preparation of this document.

Condo Documents — As you prepare to sell your condo, you should gather all condominium documents, including rules and regulations, master deed, certificate of insurance and any other paperwork that may be available from your condominium association or property management company. In addition, lenders frequently require copies of the Condominium's Operating Budget, Annual Audited Financial Statements, Monthly Financial Statements and the Condominium Association's Meeting Minutes.

A potential buyer usually wants to review these documents before making an offer, and the buyer's lender will require copies prior to issuing a mortgage commitment. Having them available to potential buyers at the beginning will help to speed up the process.

Be aware that **selling a condo is very different than selling a single family home.** For example, many lenders will not grant mortgages to new buyers if a certain percentage of units in the complex are owned by the same individual, indicating they are probably "rental" units.

PART II

Home Buyers

(12) HOMEFINDING OBJECTIVES

A home is one of the largest investments most people make. Your search for a new home will be an exciting and emotional time; but if planned well, you'll end up finding a *house* you will be happy and proud to call *home*—at a fair price with no hassle.

This *Home Buyers* section describes the steps involved in purchasing a home; from planning a focused, productive search, to making an offer, securing the right mortgage, and preparing for and attending the closing. I hope you find it informative and helpful in achieving what I recommend as your...

Homefinding Objectives

- Finding the right home at a fair price.
- Securing the right mortgage at an attractive rate.
- Both in a reasonable amount of time, and
- At a reasonable cost.

(13) GETTING STARTED RIGHT

Because buying and financing real estate today are so interrelated, involving a number of critical processes, I believe your homefinding needs are best served by a real estate professional working hand-in-hand with a mortgage professional. Both of these professionals should work together to help you achieve your homefinding objectives, while protecting and promoting your best interests.

I recommend that you start the process with a phone call to the mortgage professional, who should provide you up-to-the-minute information on the market, answer your questions, and help you identify the mortgage options that best suit your unique needs. Once this is determined, you will be advised as to exactly how much a lender is willing to lend you.

It's very important that you know this figure so you can focus your search on homes you can afford. Your mortgage professional should work with you to generate your pre-approval letter that outlines the type of mortgage you will be seeking and the maximum amount of the loan. See *Exhibit B3* on page 112. Now you are truly ready to start your search for a home.

Your New Home Wish List

Your agent should guide you through a discussion about the type of home you are looking for. This is your opportunity to outline everything you would like in your new home. This will help your agent have a clear understanding of your needs and desires to ensure that your search is well focused and productive.

Your Customized MLS Search

Your agent should develop a customized search of all the homes currently listed in the local MLS (Multiple Listing Service) based on your wish list. Both you and your agent should receive search updates by e-mail so you'll be alerted when properties come on the market that meet your criteria. In most areas, these updates not only provide plenty of details about each property, but they also contain photographs as well.

Showings

After you have had a chance to review your MLS search results, you will most likely have a list of properties that interest you. If it's convenient, you may want to take a drive by the properties to decide if the neighborhood suits you. However, try not to pass judgment on the home itself until you have had a chance to inspect it in person.

Next, contact your agent to schedule a time to see the homes that interest you. It is important to allow at least 24 hours for scheduling the showings; most sellers require a call to schedule a showing appointment time. Also, by respecting the seller's time, you are helping set the stage for future negotiations if you decide to make an offer. It is important to be on time or a little early when meeting with your agent to view the homes that have been scheduled. Your agent will have scheduled a certain amount of time for each showing, including travel time between listings, and the sellers will be expecting you at the scheduled time.

Open Houses

During the course of your new home search you may come upon an *Open House* at a property that might fit your needs, even though you haven't received word of it through your Customized MLS Search and/or your agent. If you know in advance that you are going to visit an Open House, it is best to let your agent know so that he or she can call ahead to let the listing agent know that you are coming.

In order to avoid confusion, give your agent's business card to the listing agent conducting the Open House and advise that your agent represents you as buyers regarding this property. If there is a sign-in sheet, make absolutely sure to record your agent's name and telephone number on the sheet.

A True Story:
Using Technology to Buy Your New Home
For a Fair Price With No Hassle

In today's real estate market, the smart way to buy is to utilize the most modern data and technology available to research and evaluate all the major factors bearing on selecting your dream home at a fair price and in a reasonable time.

As a *real world* example I'll explain how I helped a client accomplish that objective.

Greg and Alice were looking for a home in the $350,000–$425,000 price range in three different towns. First, I gained access to MLS data on homes recently sold and currently for sale.

Through MLS, I gathered the following key market data for the three towns (combined) in the price range my clients were interested in:

	12 Months Ago	3 Months Ago	Current
Unsold Listings:	74	82	72
Sales Activity:	13	4	9
Listing Supply (months):	5.7	5.8	8.0
Avg. Sale Price:	$398.3	$396.4	$396.9
Avg. Days on Market:	161	138	153
Sale/List Price Ratio:	96.5%	96.5%	96.0%

My Initial Analysis: I told Greg and Alice that currently, in the three towns they were interested in, there were 72 single family homes for sale in their price range—a supply that had remained fairly constant year-to-year. On the other hand, current *Sales Activity* had slacked off considerably which had changed what was a "Moderate Sellers' Market" to a "Moderate Buyers' Market" with an eight-month supply of listings at the current rate of sales, making the market much more favorable for buyers over the past 3 months.

Average Days on Market—although slightly down from a year ago—it had gone up over the last three months. Again, a favorable trend for buyers. The *Sale/List Price Ratio* (the actual sale price expressed as a percentage of the last list price) had remained very constant year-to-year, meaning that the owners of the houses that did sell had finally priced them competitively, but only after 153 days on the market. Considering that 90 days is indicative of a "Balanced

Market" (buyers and sellers about equal), this unsold home inventory level is another favorable sign for buyers.

My Recommendations (based on the Market Analysis)

- Get a *Mortgage Pre-Approval Letter* before you start looking. See **Exhibit B3** on page 112.

- Your offer price for most homes on the market should not exceed 96% of the list price.

- You should make an initial deposit of $1,000 with your offer and, if accepted,

- an additional earnest money deposit, both of which should not exceed 2% of the offer price. (Usually, in a Balanced or Sellers' Market, this would be 4%–5%).

- You should have little or no resistance from the seller having them agree to a reasonable time to transfer title and for you to get a firm mortgage commitment and home inspection.

Generally speaking, the market currently favors buyers in all of the key points of negotiation described above.

A Happy Ending: Armed with the Market Analysis Data and my recommendations, Greg and Alice achieved their objectives, and didn't have to pull out *the big guns* (the market data) until the seller told them "that's a ridiculous offer." Knowledge is power. Knowledge of markets and trends gave them the power to negotiate a fair price and terms of sale—both of which they accomplished with no hassle.

(14) MAKING AN OFFER

When you have decided to make an offer on a home that meets your needs, your agent should guide you every step of the way. He or she should provide you information about recent market activity regarding similar homes recently sold and presently for sale that are in a similar price range and community. Based on this data, your agent should give you his or her opinion of what constitutes a fair offer price. However, ultimately you will make the decision on how much to offer, as well as how much higher you are willing to go if the seller presents a counter-offer.

Because it's so critical to the success of achieving your homefinding objectives, your agent should explain what market conditions currently exist, since this will directly affect three vitally important issues:

- The trend of home values
- How long homes are staying on the market
- Who has the advantage in negotiations

Sellers' Market (More Buyers Than Sellers)
If you find yourself in a Sellers' Market, the advantage goes to sellers: the value of their homes is either stable or, more likely, increasing. Their homes tend to sell quickly and they definitely have an advantage in the key areas of negotiations, such as purchase price, amount of earnest money deposit, time to close, and refusal to consider other than normal contingencies: time to secure a firm mortgage commitment and home inspection.

Buyers' Market (More Sellers Than Buyers)
The "flip side" of a Sellers' Market. Advantage goes to the buyer.

Balanced Market (Sellers and Buyers About Equal)
Home prices stable, normal home marketing time (90–120 days) and neither party has a negotiation advantage.

The Offer to Purchase

The Offer to Purchase is made in writing and will include the offer price and proposed deadlines for the home inspection, signing a Purchase & Sale (P&S) Agreement, obtaining a firm mortgage commitment, and a closing date. This date is usually 30 to 60 days from the day the offer was accepted. See **Exhibit B1**, page 108, for an example of an Offer Form.

There will also be an amount of money (usually $1,000) offered by you to the seller as a binder to show your good faith in negotiating a fair and reasonable offer; this money is refunded to you if an agreement cannot be reached. The Offer to Purchase will also outline the deposit (or earnest money) you will be placing in escrow as a show of good faith if the offer is accepted and the P&S is signed.

Your agent will present the offer to the listing agent, and possibly to the seller as well, and will then negotiate the offer based on your instructions. When the final negotiations are completed and agreement has been reached in regard to price and terms, you and the seller will have committed yourselves to certain obligations and deadlines in order to keep the process moving forward. Your main tasks at this point will be to schedule a home inspection, sign the Purchase & Sale Agreement, and contact your mortgage professional to determine the next steps for obtaining a firm and final mortgage commitment.

(15) THE HOME INSPECTION

You or your agent will have negotiated your offer contingent on a satisfactory home inspection to be completed within a certain number of days. Rest assured, home inspectors are very responsive to the needs of buyers and can schedule and complete home inspections in a timely manner. Your agent can provide you with a list of licensed home inspectors if you don't have one in mind.

Definition

The home inspection is a professional opinion of the condition of the major components and systems of the home on the day of inspection. The home inspection is not a guarantee that the house and its systems will continue to function as intended beyond the inspection, and it is not intended to be an avenue for seeking a price reduction, unless repairs are necessary and the seller declines in pay for them.

The Process

A thorough inspection usually takes 2–3 hours to complete and it is very important that you are in attendance. The inspector will generate an inspection report either at the end of the inspection, or shortly thereafter. Either way, you will have a better understanding of the results if you accompany the inspector throughout the inspection. See example of an *Inspection Report* in **Exhibit B2** on page 110.

What's Inspected?

The home inspector will inspect anything that can be reasonably seen or accessed. The inspector cannot cut into walls or cause intentional damage during the course of an inspection to gain access to otherwise inaccessible areas of a home. The inspector also does not have a crystal ball to see into the future because the overall condition of a home and its systems are directly related to the ongoing maintenance, or lack thereof, by the owner.

The inspector will find problems or deficits with the house — no house is perfect, including many newly built homes. Structural, electrical, plumbing, or heating and ventilation problems that the seller was unaware of may be found by the inspector. In some cases, the inspector may identify items, like a stove or dishwasher that have exceeded their *useful life*. This does not mean these items don't work or that the seller should replace them — it just means they are old. In cases where a repair needs to be made to the home, the inspector is prohibited by regulation from offering estimates of repair costs. In this case, you should seek to have additional inspections by a properly licensed specialists to estimate repair costs.

When Expensive Repairs Are Indicated

Normal wear and tear notwithstanding, if a home needs a repair of significant cost, and especially if the repair will include cosmetic work, it may be better to seek a price reduction or a credit at closing and undertake the repair yourself after closing to ensure that the repair is done to your specifications with a contractor of your choosing.

(16) THE PURCHASE & SALE AGREEMENT

The Purchase & Sale Agreement (commonly referred to as the *P&S*) is a legal document that establishes binding obligations between the seller and the buyer. A typical P&S addresses at least 29 separate subjects, including the elements of the signed and accepted Offer to Purchase, which will be incorporated into this document. (See **Exhibit A2** on page 91 for an example of a P&S)

The P&S is usually generated by the listing agent and then forwarded to your agent for distribution to you and/or your real estate attorney for review. Any questions regarding the legal issues addressed in the P&S should be answered by your attorney. Although your agent may have a clear understanding of the elements of a standard P&S, he or she is not an attorney and is prohibited from offering legal advice or opinion.

The P&S is typically signed shortly after the seller accepts your offer. When you sign the P&S, you are expected to make an additional deposit (so-called *earnest money*) as a show of good faith and to demonstrate your intention to follow through with the sale. The amount of the deposit will have been established in the Offer to Purchase and typically is an amount equal to the total commission due. These funds will be placed in an escrow account (usually the listing broker's or the escrow company's) and these funds will remain in escrow until the closing. In the event that the closing does not occur, the funds cannot be released until both parties have agreed to the disposition of the funds in accordance with the terms and conditions set forth in the P&S.

(17) MORTGAGE PROGRAMS

The following describes three of the most popular types of mortgages:

Fixed Rate Mortgage — This is a mortgage where the interest rate and payments stay the same throughout the term of the loan. Fixed rate mortgages are the most stable of loan programs and are a good choice for borrowers intent on occupying the property for an extended length of time. They are available in various terms with 30 years being the most popular followed by the 15 year mortgage.

Adjustable Rate Mortgage (ARM) — These are loans where the interest rate changes periodically, usually in relation to an index, and payments may go up or down accordingly. An ARM can be an excellent choice when interest rates on fixed rate mortgages are high or for borrowers expecting to stay in their property for only a short time. Each ARM has five basic components:

- **Adjustment Period** — This is the time between changes in the interest rate and/or monthly payment. Short term ARM's will adjust monthly, every six months, or every year. Hybrid ARM's have an initial fixed period, usually 3, 5, 7, or 10 years, then adjust annually thereafter.

- **Initial Interest Rate** — Depending of the type of ARM, the initial rate is typically 0.5%–2.5% lower than that of most fixed rate mortgages.

- **Index** — The interest rate on an ARM is determined by two components: the index and the margin. Lenders base ARM rates on a variety of indexes. Some of the most common indexes used are the 1-year Constant-Maturity Treasury (CMT) securities, the Cost of Funds Index (COFI), and the London Interbank Offered Rate (LIBOR).

- **Margin** — The amount added to the index at the time of each adjustment to determine what the new interest rate will be. While the index is the variable component, the margin will always stay the same. Margins are typically between 2.25%–2.75%.

- **Interest Rate Caps** — These are consumer safeguards which place a limit on the amount that the interest rate may change. Each ARM has two caps, periodic adjustment caps and lifetime caps. Periodic adjustment caps limit the amount the interest rate can go up or down from one adjustment period to the next after the first adjustment. Some intermediate ARM's allow a larger rate change at the first adjustment and then apply a periodic adjustment cap to all future adjustments. Lifetime caps limit the amount of increase over the life of the loan. By law, virtually all ARM's must have a lifetime cap.

Reverse Mortgage (HUD definition as of 10/31/2014)

"A *reverse mortgage* is a loan for senior homeowners that uses the home's equity as collateral. The loan generally does not have to be repaid until the last surviving homeowner permanently moves out of the property or passes away. At that time, the estate has approximately six months to repay the balance of the reverse mortgage or sell the home to pay off the balance. Any remaining equity is inherited by the estate. The estate is not personally liable if the home sells for less than the balance of the reverse mortgage."

This is a highly summarized definition; you should be aware that these mortgages are not for everyone, and there are many special or unique aspects of these mortgages that should be clearly understood before applying for such a mortgage. Especially important is the fact that the borrower is obligated to maintain the property and pay the property taxes and homeowner's insurance policy premiums.

The President of the National Reverse Mortgage Lenders Association said this: "To a lot of people, a reverse mortgage is a loan of last resort for seniors without any other options. But a reverse mortgage can be a useful part of a retirement plan. However, you shouldn't use it as a bailout."

For full particulars on reverse mortgages, search *HUD Reverse Mortgage*.

(18) THE MORTGAGE PROCESS

When you apply for a mortgage loan, the lender will initiate a process to evaluate your application. This process is called underwriting. In underwriting your loan, lenders consider different factors to determine whether or not you will be approved. These factors include your income, credit rating, assets and liabilities, down payment, and the property itself. Depending on which program you may be applying for, you will be asked for documentation to help in the underwriting decision. For most loans, you will be asked to provide the following:

- A copy of your most recent pay stub
- Copies of your W-2 forms for the last two years or tax returns if self-employed
- The most recent statements on all asset accounts, including bank accounts, mutual funds, 401K plans, and retirement accounts
- The monthly payments and balances on all current liabilities such as car loans, student loans, mortgages, and credit cards

Some loan scenarios may result in additional documentation requests by the lender. Providing all documentation prior to submission of your loan to underwriting not only speeds up the process, but can also make for a faster, cleaner approval.

(19) MORTGAGE UNDERWRITING

In reviewing any loan application for approval, a set of guidelines—specific to the program applied for—is used to determine an applicant's ability to repay the loan. These standards are based upon the amount a homeowner can reasonably afford in order to own the home while taking care of other monthly obligations. This debt-to-income ratio, along with the following factors, are used to evaluate each loan.

Income

The first step of this analysis is to determine your gross stable monthly income. This includes salary, consistent bonuses, commissions, and overtime pay. Other sources of income such as pensions, child support, and social security may also be considered.

For self-employed individuals, the net profit (or loss), with depreciation expense added back in, is averaged for the prior two years to determine monthly income. A profit and loss statement for the current year may also be required but is typically not used in averaging the income.

Credit

An evaluation of your current credit report will be a major factor in determining not only if you get approved, but also the programs for which you qualify and the interest rate you are charged. A tri-merged credit report will be run showing all of your accounts as reported by the three major credit bureaus (Experian, Equifax, and TransUnion). Each of these bureaus will also assign you a credit score. Credit scores range from 300–850 and are determined using these main factors:

- **Delinquencies** — Payments which are made more than 30 days past due will show as a negative on your credit report and lower your credit score. The bigger the obligation for which you are late, the more damaging it is to your score. For example, a 30-day late payment on a mortgage or installment loan is worse than a 30-day late payment on a credit card. Also, the longer you are past due, the more adverse your score becomes. Accounts that are late 60 days, 90 days, or go into collection are very damaging to your credit score.

- **Balances** — There will be a negative impact on your credit score if your account balances are all near or at their limits. Keeping your balances at half their limit or less will improve your scores. Additionally, when paying off a credit card in full, do not close out the account. This will increase your overall available credit and help your scores.

- **Length of Credit History** — Borrowers who have had credit for a longer period of time are considered less risky than someone with a shorter credit history.

- **Inquiries** — Multiple requests for credit over a short period of time can result in a decrease in your credit scores.

For underwriting purposes, the lenders will use the borrower's middle credit score. A score of 720 or higher is considered excellent and will likely qualify for the best rates. Scores from 680–720 are considered very good and those borrowers will get standard rates on most programs. Scores from 620–680 are considered good, but rates or fees may be slightly higher on some programs in this range. Borrowers with scores below 620 are considered to be risky. They will be limited in the programs for which they qualify, and are likely to pay a higher interest rate.

Assets and Liabilities

When analyzing a loan, an underwriter will look at all assets accumulated by the borrower. These include bank accounts, retirement accounts, mutual funds, stocks and bonds and other investments. Any large deposits made into an account over the preceding 60 days will require documentation as to the source.

Liabilities for the borrower will also be analyzed by the underwriter. For any mortgages currently held, the borrower will need to document the amount of the real estate taxes and homeowners insurance along with the principal and interest. Monthly payments on installment loans will be used with the exception of loans with 10 payments or less remaining. Typically, 401K loans are not counted when calculating the borrower's monthly obligations. For revolving (credit card) debt, the minimum monthly payment required on the account — not the balance — is used for qualification purposes.

Down Payment

Another important factor in reaching the loan decision is the amount and source of your down payment. Experience has shown that the amount of the down payment is the single most important determinant of the risk characteristics of a loan. In other words, the larger your cash investment, the less likely you will be to default on your loan and lose your investment.

The source of the down payment is also important. Savings and proceeds from the sale of your present home are the most common sources for these funds. Gifts from relatives are also common, but if you use a gift as part of your down payment, documentation is required from the donor stating the funds need not be repaid. Whomever is granting the gift should be aware of the impact of current gift tax regulations.

Property Value

The lender will also order an appraisal of the property being purchased to estimate its fair market value. The property's value is determined by an independent appraiser to objectively ensure that the value of the property is sufficient to satisfy the loan.

In determining the fair market value of the property, the appraiser evaluates many factors including:

- The physical condition of the home
- The location of the home and the characteristics of the neighborhood in which it is located
- The sale price of homes recently sold which are similar to the one you have purchased

20 OTHER IMPORTANT MORTGAGE MATTERS

Rate Lock Options

There are two broad types of rate lock options:

Floating Rate — The rate is not set ("locked in") by the lender at time of application. The borrower may choose to lock the rate at any time until just prior to closing. In this sense, you *play the market.* If rates stay the same or go down, you're a winner. However, if rates rise you end up with the higher rate.

Locked Rate — The rate quoted at the time of application will be "locked-in" by the lender for a guaranteed period (usually 30–60 days).

Mortgage Insurance

Private mortgage insurance is required when your mortgage exceeds 80% of the lesser of the purchase price or appraised value of your home. The less equity you have, the more expensive the mortgage insurance.

As an alternative to traditional private mortgage insurance, many lenders now offer Lender Paid Mortgage Insurance (LPMI). For a higher interest rate on the loan or a one time upfront fee, the private mortgage insurance is not required.

Property Insurance

You must provide a homeowners insurance policy prior to closing with the amount of coverage equal to or greater than the replacement value of the property; but as a minimum, no less than the amount of the mortgage.

Escrow Accounts

Many mortgages require that funds be escrowed in advance for real estate taxes and property insurance. This escrow amount is included in your monthly payment, and the lender then pays the taxing authority and property insurer directly.

(21) PREPARING FOR THE CLOSING

At this point, your agent should have completed most of his or her duties for you. Most of your communication will now be with your mortgage professional and the person that is handling the closing—be it an attorney or escrow company closer. However, there are some other things you will need to do during this time.

Utilities

You will need to call all the applicable public utilities (electric, gas, phone, cable) to set up accounts and to help ensure that the utilities are on and in your name as of the closing date. Additionally, if the house is heated by oil, you will need to make arrangements for oil delivery. Contact landscapers and pool maintenance companies if necessary. And most importantly, don't forget to schedule the movers. You probably will not be able to bring your household goods into your new house before the closing, so plan accordingly with the movers.

Preparing the Deed

A new deed will be prepared by either the seller's attorney or the attorney that is handling the closing or, in some states, by the escrow company. You may be consulted if there are any questions as to how the title to the property will be held.

Final Walk-Thru

Within 24 hours before the closing, you should walk through the house one last time to make sure that the sellers have removed all their belongings, and that they have left behind anything specified in the P&S.

What To Bring To The Closing

- A valid driver's license or other government issued identification

- Your Social Security Number(s)

- A bank check as specified by the closing attorney

- Your checkbook in case there are any miscellaneous costs or fees

And Please Remember...

- Before going to the closing *always* call the closing attorney or escrow company to verify that the closing is still on schedule.

- All parties named on the Deed and Mortgage must be present at the closing (with proof of identification) unless other arrangements (such as granting Power of Attorney) have been made and the closing attorney or escrow company has been made aware of these arrangements.

Time Is Of The Essence

From the moment you sign the Offer to Purchase until the closing, you will be committing yourself to meeting certain deadlines, and you will be agreeing to certain penalties if deadlines are not met. It is vitally important that you take a pro-active approach to everything that needs to be completed during this period. The transaction will go much more smoothly and amicably if you meet your obligations on time, or better yet, early. If you find you cannot meet a deadline due to forces beyond your control, ask your agent to seek an extension. Don't ever wait until the deadline day.

(22) FORMS OF OWNERSHIP

Prior to closing on your new home, an attorney (typically the seller's attorney) will prepare a deed to be signed by both parties at the closing. This document will transfer to you, as the buyer, whatever interest or title the seller may have in the property at the time of the closing. When preparing the deed, the attorney will need to know in advance what form of ownership you want. You will find below a highly summarized overview of the most common forms of real estate ownership. You should consult your attorney to determine the best type of ownership for your particular circumstances.

Tenancy by the Entirety — A type of joint tenancy that provides right of survivorship and is available only to a husband and wife. Neither can sell his or her share without destroying the tenancy by the entirety.

Joint Tenancy — A form of co-ownership that gives each owner equal interest and equal rights in the property, including the right of survivorship. A joint tenant can sell his or her share, in which event the purchaser becomes a tenant in common with the other joint tenant.

Estate in Common (also known as **Tenancy in Common**) — With some exceptions, this is the presumed form of real estate ownership when a deed is conveyed to two or more people, unless another form of ownership (joint tenancy, tenancy by the entirety, or partnership) is stated in the conveying deed. This is a type of ownership without the right of survivorship.

(23) FIRST TIME HOME BUYERS

Be flexible and open to considering a number of communities and a variety of styles of homes. As a first time buyer, you are likely to have limited funds and may not be able to find a home with every feature you would like.

Consider buying a smaller home in great condition and in a great location instead of a larger fixer-upper in a marginal location. At this point, you should keep in mind that you are likely to want to move up to a larger home later on, so ease of re-sale should factor into your decision.

If you decide to buy a fixer-upper, don't underestimate the costs involved in renovation, and don't overestimate your handyman skills. The quality of the materials and craftsmanship (good or bad) will have a direct impact, either positive or negative, should you decide to sell in the future.

The purchase of a home will likely involve the purchase of some appliances and possibly some furniture; be sure to budget accordingly.

Avoid making large purchases, like a new car, or opening new lines of credit, like a furniture store charge account, after you have received your mortgage pre-approval, and especially after you have signed the Purchase & Sale Agreement (P&S). Your lender is likely to run a second credit check just prior to approving your loan. Big changes to your monthly expenses could jeopardize your loan approval.

(24) WHEN BUYING AND SELLING

If you find your dream home, but have to sell your current home to complete the purchase, you should make your sell/buy plans based on the lowest selling price you and your agent can reasonably determine for your property. Frequently seller/buyers will overprice their home because they need a certain price to buy the next home. Here's the reality: you will be hard pressed to find a buyer willing to overpay you for your current home so you can afford to buy your dream house. If you find yourself in this situation, it is best to price your home just under the price of other similar properties for sale in order to achieve a quicker sale.

In a Buyers' Market you may be able to make an offer to purchase contingent on the sale of your current home. In this type of market a seller may be happy to at least have an offer. The seller's agent will likely negotiate a "kick-out clause" into this type of offer, giving you a period of time (usually 24 hours) to remove the home sale contingency if another buyer without a house to sell makes an offer. Also, you should not accept an offer to purchase on your current home that includes a home sale contingency, as there could be a domino effect if transactions start falling apart.

In a Sellers' Market you probably won't to be able to negotiate a home sale contingency into an Offer to Purchase. Your options will include seeking a Bridge Loan, or owning two properties with two separate loans. Obviously, you will need to have the financial resources necessary to exercise either of these options.

If you have a private sewerage system (cesspool and/or septic system) at your current home, you will need to have it professionally inspected as required by most states and/or municipal regulations. If the system doesn't pass inspection, you are likely to have to repair or replace the system prior to closing. This could become a significant cost that could affect your ability to buy another home. Get the system inspected right away, and keep in mind that replacing a septic system can be a lengthy process and requires engineering and design, percolation testing of the land, local Health Department approval, and finally, installation of the new system.

Sometimes, if the buyer agrees to assume the responsibility of installing a new private sewerage system, the sale price is adjusted downward by the estimated price of the system. In this event the buyer's mortgage lender will likely require a hold-back of mortgage funds (to cover the estimated cost) until the work is completed and approved by the local municipality.

PART III

Home Sellers
— and —
Buyers

(25) THE PRINCIPAL-AGENT RELATIONSHIP

Once a home seller signs a listing agreement with a real estate broker—in which the seller agrees to pay a commission if the property is sold—that seller and broker have entered into a Principal-Agent Relationship.

Under this broad body of law, the seller's agent (the broker) has the following obligations to the seller/client: Obedience, Loyalty, Good Faith, Judgment, Prudence and Skill, Duty to Account, Duty to Personally Perform, and Duty to Give Notice. Simply stated, the agent is obligated to protect and promote the seller's best interests as if they were the agent's own.

When the agent places the seller's home for sale in the local MLS (Multiple Listing Service) and a MLS broker produces a buyer for the property, that broker is acting in a "sub-agency" position. Therefore, under these circumstances, the seller's agent is obligated to make sure that the sub-agent producing the buyer is doing nothing to endanger the agent's responsibility to protect and promote the client's best interests. In this case, the sub-agent is also required to act in a fiduciary capacity on behalf of the seller; i.e., involving confidence and trust.

It should be noted that if the MLS broker producing the buyer has been hired by the buyer to represent them (*Buyer Broker*), that broker must immediately disclose such fact to the listing broker. Then the listing broker will notify the seller of this situation and advise that the buyer will pay their broker a fee or commission directly (usually half of the gross commission). This leaves the seller usually paying the other half of the gross commission to the listing broker. Buyer brokers have the same Principal-Agent Relationship with their clients (the buyers) as listing brokers have with their clients (the sellers).

26 ABOUT REAL ESTATE COMMISSIONS

Although real estate commissions are negotiable under the law, when a home seller signs an exclusive listing agreement with a traditional real estate broker, in most cases the seller is normally bound to pay a commission of 5%–6% of the home's selling price, regardless of who sells the home—even if it turns out to be the seller. For a home that sells for $350,000, that would cost the owner $17,500–$21,000.

What does the seller normally get for this commission? The broker assumes full control of the home selling process and provides a service package that normally includes: advice on setting list price, placing a "For Sale" sign on the property, listing the property in the MLS and on the broker's web site (if they have one), handling property showings and open houses, overseeing negotiations with buyers, and coordinating the closing process.

In most cases, when the seller's home is listed on the MLS, the listing broker who listed the home usually gets 50% of the gross commission and the selling broker who produces the buyer gets the other half. The listing broker can also be the selling broker, capturing the entire commission. When there are extreme sellers' or buyers' markets, many MLS member brokers will change the split to reflect such markets. For example, in an intense sellers' market (many more buyers than sellers) the commission split might be 40% to the listing broker and 60% to the selling broker, reflecting more effort required on the selling side.

27 WHAT IS MLS? WHO ARE REALTORS

MLS stands for Multiple Listing Service, which in turn is a generic term that refers to the hundreds of individual listing services serving local markets throughout the country. The MLS provides real estate firm members with a convenient way to share information about their listings with other member firms in their local markets. Additionally, MLS systems provide detailed data on homes recently sold and currently for sale.

In the MLS, the listing broker specifies (a) the amount of the commission the seller has agreed to pay (for example, 5% of the sale price), and (b) the commission split; i.e., if and when the house sells, how much of the commission goes to the listing broker who listed the home and how much to the selling broker who produced the buyer. The traditional split is 50/50; that is, the listing broker gets 2.5% and the selling broker also gets 2.5%.

Many MLS's are owned and operated by local Realtor boards, though there are some that are owned by independent companies. MLS's are membership based, limited primarily to real estate brokers.

Realtors are members of the National Association of Realtors (NAR) who subscribe to a Code of Ethics and Standards of Practice, including Duties to Clients and Customers, the Public, and their fellow Realtors. NAR created Realtor.com, currently the largest supplier of real estate listings nationally.

(28) THE REAL ESTATE MARKET

There are economic events that can occur in every market area that can impact the value and marketability of a home, either positively or negatively. Consider: national recession or expansion, regional unemployment rates and trends, a depressed metropolitan area dependent on one industry, a major employer leaving a suburban market, big tax increase in a community, a new waste disposal plant in a neighborhood. The list is endless—and dynamic.

The Most Important Market Factor

However, by far the single biggest market impact is national—affecting all markets—and that is the credit market. The timing here is critical. When the Federal Reserve dropped the base rate to near zero in 2002—and kept it at a low level for some time—we had a national Sellers' Market like we've never had before. Demand for houses soared, supplies dwindled and, as a result, home values started to rise. In the early stages of this easy, cheap money, renters could suddenly afford to become buyers at the bottom of the single-family housing food chain. The sellers of these lower priced homes suddenly were able to upscale and on and on up the chain, pushing demand and prices up and up.

Boom and Bust

Historically, each real estate boom has ultimately become a bust to some degree. What goes up in real estate usually goes down. The degree of "down" almost always depends on the intensity and corresponding speed of price increases on the "up" side. Generally, if the up side is gradual, the down side will be slight or mild. However, if that up side was fast and intense with big, rapid price increases, the odds are that the down side will likely mirror it. So it's safe to say that the real estate market is dynamic, and directly impacts home sellers and buyers. It's important to understand that the current market has a very direct impact on home values, marketing time, cost of sale, and negotiation advantage. Generally, real estate markets can be defined at any given time as falling into one of five broad categories as described in the *Introduction* on page 7.

(29) FIXTURES VS. PERSONAL PROPERTY

Having a clear understanding of these subjects will help sellers and buyers avoid potential problems during the negotiating phase, and even after title is transferred.

Fixtures: A fixture is an item of personal property that is so affixed or attached to the dwelling that it loses its character as personal property and becomes a part of the real estate. Wall-to-wall carpeting, television antennas, ceiling fans, lighting fixtures and built-in appliances are considered permanent fixtures, assumed to be included in the sale price, and listed in the P&S.

Personal Property: On the other hand, the seller may decide to leave behind and attempt to sell certain items of personal property when they vacate, such as custom-made draperies, washer, dryer and the like. If this is the case, the sellers should make sure to advise their agent of their intent. Usually, the addition of personal property to the seller's offering does not add a significant amount to value, but there are exceptions.

(30) LOCAL ORDINANCES

What You Need to Know About
Carbon Monoxide Detectors

Most states and/or municipalities require carbon monoxide detectors in any residence that contains fossil-fuel burning equipment (furnace, boiler, water heater, fireplace or other device) or that has an attached garage. As with smoke detector requirements, this law is usually enforced by the local fire department during its inspection prior to the sale or transfer of property.

What You Need to Know About
Smoke Detectors

Most states and/or municipalities require that buildings or structures occupied in whole or in part for residential purposes must, upon the sale or transfer of such building or structure, be equipped by the seller with approved smoke detectors. Usually, local fire departments enforce the provisions of this law. If you are selling your home you need to contact your local fire department to discuss the specific regulations for your community, the fee you will pay, and to schedule an inspection.

Make sure your real estate agent advises you of any other ordinances that may impact you.

(31) FAIR HOUSING LAW

The Fair Housing Law declares that it is illegal to discriminate on the basis of Race, Color, Religious Creed, National Origin, Sex, Sexual Orientation, Age, Children, Ancestry, Marital Status, Veteran History, Public Assistance Recipient, or Handicap (Mental or Physical). It is unlawful practice for owners, lessees, sub-lessees, licensed real estate brokers, assignees, managing agents, or unit owners to refuse (on the basis of membership in one or more of the above groups) the:

- Right to Buy
- Right to Lease
- Right to Rent
- Right of Ownership
- Right of Possession

Under the law of most states, it is Illegal to:

- Discourage a person from buying or renting a dwelling in a particular area and encourage him or her to buy or rent in another area.

- Represent that a dwelling is not available for sale, rent or inspection when the dwelling is, in fact, so available.

- Charge or quote a higher rental or sale price for a dwelling.

- State or provide less favorable terms for the rental or sale of a dwelling.

- Publish discriminatory advertising.

- Discriminate in the granting of mortgage loans.

- Discriminate on the basis of a rental subsidy recipient by refusing to make reasonable accommodations in policies and services or refusing to permit reasonable modifications of dwellings.

- Discriminate on the basis of a rental subsidy recipient by refusing to rent to subsidy recipients because of subsidy program requirements.

- Refuse to rent to families with children under six because of lead paint which, in most states, must be removed prior to rental or sale.

PART IV

Cyclical
Market Issues

CYCLICAL MARKET ISSUES

A brief history of what led to the three issues addressed in this section:

Their genesis really started when the Federal Reserve dropped the base interest rate to near zero in 2002—and kept it at a low level for an extended period of time. This resulted in a national Sellers' Market like we've never experienced before. Demand for houses soared, supplies dwindled and, as a result, home values started to skyrocket. Adding fuel to the fire, our federal government—through Fannie Mae and Freddie Mac—pressured lenders to finance *affordable housing* with very weak underwriting standards, and took into their inventory hundreds of thousands of sub-prime (and below sub--prime) mortgages with unverified statements of borrowers' debts, incomes and credit-worthiness.

Demand for housing soared, supplies dwindled and, as a result, home values started to rapidly rise. In the early stages of this easy, cheap mortgage money, renters could suddenly afford to become buyers at the bottom of the single-family housing food chain. The sellers of these lower priced homes suddenly were able to upscale—and on and on up the housing chain, pushing demand and prices up and up.

Then the bubble burst in the latter part of 2008 when it became apparent to the financial world that the millions of mortgages written during this period—packaged as mortgage-backed securities, and sold to thousands of investors and institutions—were hardly worth the paper they were written on.

In my opinion, the **blame** for this huge financial debacle rests with our federal government, whose politicians wanted to further enhance their political capital by promising and legislating a home for everyone, whether or not they could afford it.

The **responsibility** rests with Wall Street, who will always find a way to sell any financial product, particularly those underwritten by our federal government and paid for by us taxpayers.

(32) UNDERWATER

Definition: a mortgage balance that exceeds the value of the home.

In 2012, approximately 16 million (31.4%) of U.S. homeowners with mortgages were underwater. In the first quarter of 2014, it was 9.7 million (18.8%) according to Zillow, Inc. In addition, at this same time, there were another 10 million households that didn't have enough equity in their homes, making it difficult for them to sell and have enough left over to pay the broker's fee, closing costs and a down payment on another home.

In most "underwater" cases that had their genesis during the 2002–2008 period, these homeowners either bought houses they couldn't afford at the time because of lax or non-existent mortgage underwriting standards, and/or they failed to project what might happen to the value of their homes—in relationship to their mortgages—should the market cease to continually expand upward. The ideal of any investment is to buy low and sell high. Sadly, these folks did the reverse.

Getting Level With or Above the Water

If you find yourself in this position, do not try to avoid the lender. In fact, do just the opposite. The sooner you approach your lender, the better chance you have to extract yourself from the problem with less damage than would be the case if you tried to avoid the lender.

Most lenders are open to borrowers who come forward and express a sincere commitment to do everything in their power to repay the debt.

For starters, foreclosure is very expensive, time consuming and a big distraction for lenders. So, when they know they have a problem borrower, they evaluate how *underwater* the property is and then complete a cost/benefit study. For example, let's say the current market value of the property is $300,000 (purchased four years ago for $500,000 with a $400,000 mortgage). Continuing the example, here's their usual approach:

Probable Sale Price:	$300,000
Deduct	
Holding/maintaining 12 months: $30,000	
Legal: 5,000	
Miscellaneous: 10,000	
Mortgage Balance: 380,000	
TOTAL DEDUCTIONS:	425,000
Estimated Loss by Foreclosure:	($125,000)

This is their starting point to negotiate with the borrower. There are two broad avenues the lender can explore: (1) try to work out a restructuring of the loan and/or special repayment schedule, or (2) consider a *Short Sale* approach (see *32–Short Sale* following*)*. Without going into great detail, either of these approaches is likely to be at least $45,000 less costly to the lender than going into foreclosure.

(33) SHORT SALE

Definition: The sale of a home where the proceeds from the sale will fall *short* of paying off the balance owed, and the owner cannot afford to pay the deficiency.

In practically all cases, the home is also *underwater* (as previously described). A sale becomes "short" when a lender agrees to release the owner from paying some or all of the balance on the mortgage and accepting less than the amount owed.

If you find yourself in this position, a local professional real estate agent in tune with the market conditions and lenders involved, can usually advise you as to how amenable your lender might be to a Short Sale.

You will have to prove that you have an economic and/or financial hardship for your lender to even consider a Short Sale. If a lender does consider this, it doesn't necessarily release you from an obligation to repay some or all of the deficiency. As in the case of *underwater* home owners, it's all negotiation, so I would advise that you have a qualified professional in your corner.

(34) FLIPPING

Definition: Attempting to buy homes low and sell them high in a short period of time, either in as is condition or fixed up (*fix and flip*). This objective invariably assumes a rising market, and as is the case in all financial projections, involves risk. In this case, a great deal of risk.

However, in a few cases a great deal of risk can result in a great deal of reward. Particularly if the market is rapidly improving. When *flipping*, timing is all.

Do speculators consistently achieve this objective? Not usually. In my active real estate days, I did speculate and consistently achieved this objective because I was working in my local market area with sellers and buyers every day. I could look at a house and tell you instantly what I could sell it for. My point is that to be consistently successful in the *flipping* business you must totally understand the market in which the home is located on a daily basis. As a corollary, that's why the only people who make the big money in the stock market are those who live and work in it every day.

PART V

Landlords

(35) SELECTING A LEASING FIRM

In most areas, there are numerous rental management and residential real estate firms from which to make a selection. Some deal exclusively in rental management. Others are divisions of residential real estate companies. If you have become acquainted with any real estate agents in your community, ask them if the firms they are associated with provide rental management services. You may also want to check local real estate web sites and the "Homes For Rent" classified listings in your local newspapers to check out the competition for tenants and to see which companies seem to be most active in your area.

(36) RETAINING A LEASING FIRM

If you select a rental management firm (*leasing firm*), the next step is to execute a Leasing Contract specifying the duties and responsibilities of that firm and your obligations as the property owner during the term of the contract.

The contract should include the legal description of the property (street address is usually sufficient), a list and description of the specific services to be performed by the leasing firm, and a specific time and dates for both the beginning and the termination of that firm's services. The following items should also be addressed in the contract:

Pre-Leasing Procedure

Tenant screening, rental application, credit report.

Lease Terms

The contract should include length and terms of leases with tenants who will occupy your home in your absence, including specific termination/vacate dates to assure that your property will be available and in move-in condition if you return. Also, the contract should address the amount of the monthly lease payment and the security deposit. Any restrictions, such as no smoking or no pets, should be written into the lease agreement. Rental payment, collection, and accounting procedures should also be addressed.

Inspections

Move-in, move-out inspections should be performed by the leasing firm in the presence of the tenant. Periodic inspections (at least quarterly) should also be specified, covering both the interior and exterior of your property. Results of all inspections should be reported to you and documented with photographs where appropriate.

Notification

The leasing firm should be required to notify you of any damage, loss or accidents occurring on or to your property. Such notice should be in writing and communicated in a timely fashion.

Service Contracts, Maintenance, Repairs

The contract should authorize your leasing firm to contract for specific utilities or services required for the ongoing operation, maintenance and safety of your property. Make sure to give them a list of all the service suppliers you are happy with. The contract should also spell out specific maintenance services which your leasing firm is authorized to perform or to have performed, and dollar limits for such services. Procedures for obtaining your authorization for any repairs (both ordinary and emergency) beyond those limits should be included as well.

Commissions, Fees

The management contract with the leasing firm should set forth the amounts and terms of any fees to be paid by you, including a leasing fee, a management fee, and any other fees which might be required during the term of the contract.

Hold Harmless / Insurance

The leasing firm should provide proof of general and automobile liability insurance and workmen's compensation insurance in commercially reasonable amounts. Also, ask if they have errors and omissions insurance. The contract should contain a "Hold Harmless" clause whereby the leasing firm agrees to indemnify and hold you harmless from any and all damages, losses, claims, suits or injuries arising out of or from the firm's actions or omissions in their performance of the contract.

(37) ESTIMATING RENTAL VALUE

Before advertising and exposing your home to the rental marketplace, a reference point should be established as to your home's comparative rental value.

Your leasing firm should compare your home with recent rentals of homes that are similar to yours. This analysis should take into consideration how much they are leasing for, as well as their location, age, condition and specific amenities which may add to or detract from their rental value. This approach is identical to the appraisal process used to estimate the likely selling price of a home. See *Exhibit C1* on page 114, *Rental Value Appraisal* format.

It's not uncommon for rental value estimates to contain observations such as:

- Rent could be higher if the kitchen were repainted and curled linoleum re-glued or replaced.

- Lot size is small relative to similar homes, but home does have better walking access to local schools.

■ Subject home is adjacent to large recreational area, complete with wooden playground structures. Should be worth $100 per month more than similar rentals when renting to a family with children.

The above assessments could be valuable both in preparing the home for showing and in targeting specific marketing approaches.

(38) MARKETING YOUR RENTAL

Achieving your property leasing objectives depends largely upon the successful marketing of your property to the rental marketplace. Keeping your property occupied to credit-worthy, responsible tenants is crucial to the financial success of this venture.

The Marketplace

Nothing exists in a vacuum, and the rental value of your home is no exception. There are global, regional, and neighborhood conditions which can impact rental values. Economic conditions, including cost of living and cost of housing can drive rental values. Corporate mobility and relocation patterns can impact the availability of suitable tenants. The existing supply of similar housing in your area on both a rental and purchase basis can also affect pricing. These conditions, while beyond your control, must be taken into consideration when establishing a marketing plan for your property.

Property Factors

The condition of your property is probably the single most important factor that will influence the financial success of your rental project.

Exterior. The exterior appearance of your property has a great deal to do with *rentability*. Clean fresh paint; driveway, walks, fences in good repair; trees trimmed; lawn, shrubs, landscaping in cared-for condition. All this creates what leasing agents refer to as *curb appeal*.

For purposes of both marketability and the safety and preservation of your property, the roof, gutters and downspouts should also be given the same attention. Shingles and flashing should be checked and replaced if necessary. Sidewalks, handrails, stairs, and porches should be intact and in good repair. These are some of the first impressions that prospective tenants have about your home.

Systems. Obviously, the home's mechanical systems should be in good working condition. Furnaces, heat pumps, and air conditioners should be serviced as necessary to make them as worry-free as possible during the term of the lease. Preventive servicing on a regular schedule can often help reduce the risk of emergency repair costs.

Electrical. Fixtures, outlets, and switches should be in safe operating condition. Smoke and carbon monoxide detectors should be mounted in critical locations on each floor (including attic and basement), and fresh batteries installed. Also, you or your leasing firm should review your local ordinances for any specific requirements on rental property.

Interior. The interior appearance of your home is also important. Some *spruce-up* painting to interior walls and ceilings can make a property more attractive. When repainting, consider neutral colors for greater market appeal. Wall-to-wall carpeting should be professionally cleaned; hardwood and tile floors cleaned and polished for best possible appeal.

Kitchen and Baths. Be sure all fixtures and appliances are clean and in good working condition. These rooms should be spotless.

Windows. Draperies, curtains, and blinds should be clean and attractively hung. Window treatments can add great appeal.

PART VI

Landlords
—— *and* ——
Tenants

(39) TENANT EVALUATION

While a properly constructed lease agreement is very important should problems occur during the term of the lease, the best safeguard is a good tenant evaluation program—starting with a Rental Application. See *Exhibit C2* on page 117. You or your leasing firm should employ a number of standard procedures in evaluating rental applicants:

Verification of Employment. Both current and previous employers should be contacted to verify the applicant's stability on the job and ability to make the rental payments.

Verification of Residence. Current and previous landlords should be contacted to verify the applicant's history of timely rent payments and responsible care of the premises. References from prior landlords may be more reliable, as current landlords may be interested in seeing undesirable tenants move elsewhere.

Verification of Credit. The applicant should be asked to list his or her total financial obligations including monthly payments, and to give banking and other credit references. These should be checked to verify the applicant's current outstanding obligations and credit payment history.

(40) THE LEASE AGREEMENT

The lease agreement is the key document that spells out the duties and obligations of both tenant and landlord. It lists and describes any restrictions to the tenant's occupancy. Remedies for breaches of the agreement and methods by which such remedies are applied must also be spelled out clearly as follows:

Premises

The location of the property and a description of any furnishings and/ or other personal property included in the lease should be specified in the agreement or in an attachment referenced in the agreement.

Term

The beginning and ending dates of the lease should be specified exactly in the lease, along with provisions for prorating rent, should occupancy not be available at the start of the lease or should the premises be held over, with your consent, beyond the term of the lease.

Rent

The amount and manner of payment of the monthly rent should be specified, along with provisions for a *late charge* if payments are not received in a timely fashion. The lease should also specify that if payments are not received on time, the remaining rent over the entire term is accelerated and becomes due and payable. Any payments in addition to the rent which must be paid by the tenant should also be specified in detail, including utilities, refuse collection fees, and security alarm monitoring fees.

Security Deposit

The amount of the security deposit, the manner in which the deposit will be escrowed, distribution of interest from the security escrow, and administrative fees should also be stipulated. These matters may be limited by local ordinance, so they should be carefully checked out. Inspection reports, property condition photos, and inventories should be referred to in the lease agreement and attached as *exhibits*. The terms and conditions relating to the eventual return of the security deposit should also be clearly spelled out.

Use of Premises

The lease agreement should stipulate that the tenant *shall not make or permit* any use of the leased premises beyond the specific terms of the lease, and that all such use and occupancy shall be in accordance with local laws, statutes, by-laws, rules and regulations of the municipality in which the property is located. The lease should also include specific names of those parties who will be occupying the premises and should restrict any other permanent or temporary occupancy by anyone other than those specified in the lease. Additionally, the lease should prohibit any subleasing of the premises by tenants. If pets are to be allowed, you must give your written consent as landlord. The lease should also specify that such consent can be revoked at any time and that the tenant is fully responsible for damage caused by pets in or on the property.

The lease should also include a *hold harmless* clause indemnifying you from any liability arising from the tenant's occupancy or use of the property.

Maintenance and Repairs

The lease should specify that the tenant is responsible for *preventive maintenance* required to preserve the property, keeping fixtures and furnishings in *the same good repair and condition as on the beginning date of the lease*. Normal maintenance and servicing of furnaces, air conditioners, and water conditioners should also be spelled out as tenant responsibilities. The lease should also address the tenant's responsibility for any damage that results from negligence or misuse on the part of the tenant. If any furnishings are included in the lease, they should be itemized in a separate exhibit and referred to in the agreement. In this event, the tenant's responsibility for maintenance and condition of furnishings should also be detailed in the lease.

Vacating

The lease should specify that the tenant may not leave the property vacant or unoccupied for more than a maximum number of days (as specified by you) without your written consent. The date, terms and conditions on which the tenant must return the leased premises to you should be specified. The lease should stipulate that the tenant's responsibilities *survive the termination of the lease agreement.*

Insurance

To protect both landlord and tenant, the lease should stipulate that it is the tenant's responsibility and obligation to obtain an insurance policy to insure his/her personal property and personal liability. Additionally, you should amend your homeowner's policy if possible and practical, or acquire specific Landlord Insurance to protect your liability and property interest while your home is vacant and/or a tenant occupies your home in your absence.

Keys, Entry, Inspections

The lease should specify that you will maintain duplicate keys to all locks and that if any locks are changed, added or replaced (only upon your prior approval), the tenant must supply you with duplicate keys. The lease should also make provisions for your rental management firm's periodic inspection of both the exterior and interior of the property and for entry (by appointment) for the purposes of showing the property during the last ninety days of the lease. If you have an alarm system, a new code should be provided the leasing firm and the tenant.

Default

The terms and conditions under which a tenant will be considered in default should be specifically addressed, as should remedies that will be applied under such circumstances.

(41) VACATING/OCCUPANCY

When you move out of your home, the rental management firm should prepare a checklist indicating the condition in which you are turning the property over to them. The leasing agent should conduct a walk-through with you, indicating any visible damage and notable signs of wear and tear. The report should be accompanied by photos where appropriate.

This report will also serve as the *Condition of Premises Inventory* which the tenant will sign upon occupancy as an addendum to the lease agreement. The proper operation of all mechanical systems should also be verified at this time; if any are in question, a competent service technician or inspector's opinion should be obtained and included in the report.

Most rental management experts recommend that residences be rented unfurnished. If, however, you wish to include furnishings in the lease, a separate inventory should be developed, noting visible damage or signs of wear, supported with photos where appropriate.

Note: Homeowners who opt to lease their homes furnished should accept the fact that even with normal use and care, furnishings may show considerable wear and tear by the end of the lease period. Your furnishings likely will not look the same to you upon your return, even under the best of conditions.

(42) AFTER THE TENANT MOVES IN

The *Condition of Premises Inventory* (and the *Condition of Furnishings Inventory*, if applicable) should be signed by the tenant and appended to the lease agreement.

Collection of the monthly rent should be the responsibility of your leasing firm, and the lease should specify that payments must be received at that firm's address on or before the first day of each month. The agreement should also specify a late payment that will be due should the rent deadline be missed.

When a tenant fails to pay rent on time, your rental management firm has the right to notify the tenant that the remaining rent over the entire term is accelerated and becomes due and payable. However, before eviction proceedings are instituted against a tenant for lack of payment or for any other reason, the leasing firm should make every effort to allow the tenant to make up the rent deficiency or to correct any other problem that may exist. It is important that your rental management firm try to resolve problems directly with the tenant in this manner, as eviction proceedings and the resultant loss of rent can be very expensive and time-consuming.

Repair Management

From time to time it may be necessary for your rental management firm to hire contractors to perform routine or special maintenance or repairs, either to protect the physical well-being of your home or to prevent harm to a tenant due to a problem in your home. Your leasing firm will select contractors (whom you have recommended), review their bids and estimates, and inspect work performed before issuing payment whenever repairs or routine maintenance are required. If you have any service contractors (plumbers, electricians) with whom you have already established a good working relationship, give their names to your rental management firm with instructions to use them whenever such services are needed.

You should set a dollar limit beyond which your prior personal approval will be required before any repairs are authorized. However, there should be a provision to handle emergency repairs without the delay of such authorizations when they are necessary to protect the property and/or to prevent personal injury to anyone on the premises.

Periodic Inspections and Reports

Your leasing firm should perform periodic inspections of the general condition and appearance of your property. Should any conditions be noted that may indicate an interior problem, the leasing agent will make an appointment with the tenant to inspect the interior of the home. Any examination of the interior of the home during the term of the lease must be handled in a sensitive manner, as tenants are entitled to *quiet enjoyment* of the home. Any unwarranted and/or unannounced intrusion by you or your leasing agent would be considered improper.

Your leasing firm should also provide an accounting of all income and expenses and current account balance on at least a semi-annual basis. Any unusual expenses which might be anticipated during the next accounting period should be noted at this time; for example, an increase in taxes, insurance, assessments, or necessary repairs noted in inspections.

(43) WHEN THE TENANT MOVES OUT

Upon the expiration of a lease, your rental management firm will perform a thorough inspection of the property, comparing the condition of the home with that noted on the original *Condition of Premises Inventory*, and the *Condition of Furnishings Inventory*, if applicable.

Should damage be noted that seems beyond what might be considered *ordinary wear and tear*, an amount necessary to correct the damage will be withheld from the tenant's security deposit. Pursuing any damage claims in excess of the tenant's security deposit will likely require legal action, although by scheduling regular interior inspections of your property during the lease term, your rental management firm is greatly reducing the probability of encountering any costly surprises at the time of the tenant's vacating.

The date for the tenant's move-out should be coordinated with the date you expect to move back in or re-lease, if appropriate. Should this date change to a date other than originally anticipated, your rental management firm may be able to execute an extension of the lease for a specific period of time or on a month-to-month basis.

If you're going to re-lease, it is important that your leasing firm closely coordinates the changeover in tenancy. In some cases, the new tenant may be able to take occupancy immediately; in other cases, the firm may need to coordinate renovation, repair, and cleaning of the home in a timely manner in order for a new tenant to move in as soon as possible.

Exhibits

EXHIBIT A1

Home Appraisal Format

Basically, an appraisal (or estimate) of the value of a home is based on comparison—and as a result of that comparison—an adjustment to the estimate of the present value of that home is then made.

The subject home is fully described, and is then compared to similar (comparable) homes recently sold.

The example on the next page—a simplified version of a detailed appraisal done by a certified professional—is a form of an estimate of a "Range of Value" a real estate agent might complete.

The appraisal process has not changed in years. What has changed, of course, is the use of technology and home values.

For details, see: *1–Pricing Your Home* on page 12.

MARKET VALUE ANALYSIS

Owner(s): John R. and Mary L. Jones _____ Telephone: 555-5622

Subject Property (Address) 123 Maple Street, Dorval, IL 78279

Date of Inspection: October 14 _____ ☒ Occupied   ☐ Vacant

Agent: James Smith _____ Agency: Accredited Realty _____ Telephone: 555-2179

Data	Subject	Comparable Sale 1		Comparable Sale 2		Comparable Sale 3	
Address		58 Oakland Terrace Dorval		1236 Edgewood Dorval		130 Elm Street Dorval	
Distance From Subject		1 Mile		2 Miles		2 Blocks	
Original List Price		$177,500		$184,000		$172,500	
List Price at Time of Sale		$172,500		$179,000		$169,900	
Days on Market		119		123		56	
Sales Price/Closing Date		$169,500 10/5		$176,500 7/28		$165,000 9/15	
	DESCRIPTION	DESCRIPTION	+/-*	DESCRIPTION	+/-*	DESCRIPTION	+/-*
Approximate Age	5 Yrs.	4 Yrs.		3 Yrs.		8 Yrs.	-
Lot Size	120 x 180	110 x 120	-	115 x 170		115 x 165	
Location (Site / View)	Good	Good		Excellent	+	Fair	-
Architectural Style	Bi-level	Bi-level		Bi-level		2 Story	
Condition	Good	Good		Good		Average	-

Room Count	Total	BRs	Baths	Total	BRs	Baths		Total	BRs	Baths		Total	BRs	Baths	
	7	3	2	7	3	2 1/2	+	7	3	2 1/2	+	7	3	2	

	Subject	Comparable Sale 1	+/-	Comparable Sale 2	+/-	Comparable Sale 3	+/-
Approximate Sq. Ft.	2015	2025		2200	+	1850	-
Basement	Full	Full		Full		Full	
Garage	2 Car Attached	2 Car Attached		2 Car Attached		2 Car Attached	
Pool/Deck/Patio	Deck	2 Level Deck	+	Deck		None	-
Air Conditioning	✓	✓		✓		✓	
Financing/Concessions	✓	✓		✓		✓	
Special Features	1 Fireplace	None		1 Fireplace		1 Fireplace	
Overall rating of Comparable Sale compared to Subject		☐ More ☒ Equal ☐ Less Favorable		☒ More ☐ Equal ☐ Less Favorable		☐ More ☐ Equal ☒ Less Favorable	

*-Note: A plus (+) indicates the Comparable is **significantly more favorable** than Subject; a minus (-) indicates **significantly less favorable** than Subject.

Describe significant value-related differences between Subject Property and Comparable Sales:

Comparable Sale 1: Lot size is smaller and not as private as Subject's. There is no fireplace. One-half bath on lower level is a plus; two-level deck enhanced by nice landscaping.

Comparable Sale 2: Excellent location on quiet cul-de-sac,. Extra one-half bath on lower level and more square footage. Market values have depreciated slightly since July.

Comparable Sale 3: Three years older than subject. Located on busy street. Smaller in size and condition is average.

THE HOME MARKETING ANALYSIS INDICATES:

Estimated Range of Value	Most Probable Sales Price	Suggested Initial List Price
$165,000 **to** $175,000	$169,000	$174,900

EXHIBIT A2

Purchase & Sale Agreement (P&S)

The Standard Form Purchase and Sale Agreement on the next five pages is used in Massachusetts.

However, although nomenclature and process may differ a bit from state to state, they all cover essentially the subjects you see here.

When selling and/or buying a home, your real estate agent or local attorney will use the standard form of a P&S for your area.

For more background, see: *16–The Purchase & Sale Agreement* on page 44.

STANDARD FORM
PURCHASE AND SALE AGREEMENT

1. PARTIES

John and Mary Smith

hereinafter called the SELLER, agrees to SELL and

Thomas and Elizabeth Jones

hereinafter called the BUYER or PURCHASER, agrees to BUY, upon the terms hereinafter set forth

2. DESCRIPTION

The following described premises: **123 Main Street, Anytown, MA 02779** , and being more fully described in a deed recorded with Plymouth County Registry of Deeds Title reference Book **1920** , Page **73**
Said property contains 81, 893 square feet of land.

3. BUILDINGS; IMPROVEMENTS ; FIXTURES

Included in the sale as a part of said premises are the buildings, structures, and improvements now STRUCTURES, thereon, and fixtures belonging to the SELLER and used in connection therewith including, IMPROVEMENTS, if any, all wall-to-wall carpeting, drapery rods, automatic garage door openers, venetian blinds, window shades, screens, screen doors, storm windows and doors, awnings, shutters, furnaces, heaters, heating equipment, stoves, ranges, oil and gas burner and fixtures appurtenant thereto, hot water heaters, plumbing and bathroom fixtures, electric and other lighting fixtures, mantels, outside television antennas, fences, gates, trees, shrubs, plants, and if built in, air conditioning equipment, ventilators, garbage disposers, dishwashers, washing machines and driers; and but excluding

NONE

4. TITLE DEED

Said premises are to be conveyed by a good and sufficient Quitclaim deed running to the BUYER, or to the nominee designated by the BUYER by written notice to the SELLER at least seven days before the deed is to be delivered as herein provided, and said deed shall convey a good and clear record and marketable title thereto, free from encumbrances, except

(a)	Provisions of existing building and zoning laws;
(b)	Existing rights and obligations in party walls which are not the subject of written agreement;
(c)	Such taxes for the then current year as are not due and payable on the date of the delivery of such deed;
(d)	Any liens for municipal betterments assessed after the date of this agreement;
(e)	Any easement, restriction or agreement of record presently in force and applicable which do not interfere with the reasonable use of the premises as now used.
(f)	Include hereby by specific reference any restrictions, easements, rights and obligations in party walls not included in (b), leases, municipal and other liens, other encumbrances, and make provision to protect SELLER against BUYER'S breach of SELLER'S covenants in leases where necessary.

5. PLANS

If said deed refers to a plan necessary to be recorded therewith the SELLER shall deliver such plan with the deed in form adequate for recording or registration.

6. REGISTERED TITLE

In addition to the foregoing, if the title to said premises is registered, said deed shall be in form sufficient to entitle the BUYER to a Certificate of Title of said premises, and the SELLER shall deliver with said deed all instruments, if any, necessary to enable the BUYER to obtain such Certificate of Title.

7. PURCHASE PRICE

The agreed purchase price for said premises is: **TWO HUNDRED THIRTY THOUSAND DOLLARS** of which

$	50,000.00	has been paid to the herewith, and
$	180,000.00	are to be paid at the time of delivery of the deed in cash, or by certified, cashier's, treasurer's or bank check.
$	230,000.00	TOTAL

8. TIME FOR PERFORMANCE; DELIVERY OF DEED;

Such deed is to be delivered at **TWO** o'clock PM on the **12th** day of **MAY** 2010, at **Plymouth Registry of Deeds** or at the offices of the conveyancing counsel unless otherwise agreed upon in writing. It is agreed that time is of the essence of this agreement.

9 .POSSESSION and CONDITION of PREMISES.

Full possession of said premises free of all tenants and occupants, except as herein provided, is to be delivered at the time of the delivery of the deed, said premises to be then (a) in the same condition as they now are, reasonable use and wear thereof excepted, and (b) not in violation of said building and zoning laws, and (c) in compliance with the provisions of any instrument referred to in clause 4 hereof. The BUYER shall be entitled to an inspection of said premises prior to the delivery of the deed in order to determine whether the condition thereof complies with the terms of this clause. Said property review shall be made within 24 hours prior to transfer.

10. EXTENSION TO PERFECT TITLE OR MAKE PREMISES CONFORM

If the SELLER shall be unable to give title or to make conveyance, or to deliver possession of the premises, all as herein stipulated, or if at the time of the delivery of the deed the premises do not conform with the provisions hereof, SELLER shall use reasonable efforts to remove any defects in title, or the deliver possession as provided herein, or to make the said premises conform to the provisions hereof, as the case may be, in which event the SELLER shall give written notice thereof to the BUYER at or before the time for performance hereunder, and thereupon the time for performance hereof shall be extended for a period of thirty days provided BUYER can obtain a corresponding extension to his financing commitment.

11. FAILURE TO PERFECT TITLE OR MAKE PREMISES CONFORM, etc.

If at the expiration of the extended time the SELLER shall have failed so to remove any defects in title, deliver possession, or make the premises conform, as the case may be, all as herein agreed, or if at any time during the period of this agreement or any extension thereof, the holder of a mortgage on said premises shall refuse to permit the insurance proceeds, if any to be used for such purposes, then at the BUYER'S option, any payments made under this agreement shall be forthwith refunded and all other obligation of all parties hereto shall ceased and this agreement shall be void without recourse to the parties hereto.

12. BUYER'S ELECTION TO ACCEPT TITLE

The BUYER shall have the election, at either the original or any extended time for performance, to accept such title as the SELLER can deliver to the said premises in their then condition and to pay therefore the purchase price without deduction, in which case the SELLER shall convey such title, except that in the event of such conveyance in accord with the provisions of this clause, if the said premises shall have been damaged by fire or casualty insured against, then the SELLER shall, unless the SELLER has previously restored the premises to their former condition, either:

(a)   pay over or assign to the BUYER, on delivery of the deed, all amounts recovered or recoverable on account of such insurance, less any amounts reasonably expended by the SELLER for an partial restoration, or

(b)   if a holder of a mortgage on said premises shall not permit the insurance proceeds or a part thereof to be used to restore the said premises to their former condition or to be so paid over or assigned, give to the BUYER a credit against the purchase price, on delivery of the deed, equal to said amounts so recovered or recoverable and retained by the holder of the said mortgage less any amounts reasonably expended by the SELLER for any partial restoration.

13. ACCEPTANCE OF DEED

The acceptance of a deed by the BUYER or his nominee as the case may be, shall be deemed to be a full performance and discharge of every agreement and obligation herein contained or expressed, except such as are, by the terms hereof, to be performed after the delivery of said deed.

14. USE OF PURCHSE MONEY TO CLEAR TITLE

To enable the SELLER to make conveyance as herein provided, the SELLER may, at the time of delivery of the deed, use the purchase money or any portion thereof to clear the title of any or all encumbrances or interests, provided that provisions for prompt recording thereof in accordance with prevailing conveyancing practices made at the time of closing.

15. MORTGAGE CONTINGENCY CLAUSE

In order to help finance the acquisition of said premises, the BUYER shall apply for a conventional bank or other institutional mortgage loan of **$180,000.00** at prevailing rates, terms and conditions. If despite the BUYER'S diligent efforts, a commitment for such loan cannot be obtained on or before **April 30, 2010** the BUYER may terminate this agreement by written notice to the SELLER and/or the Broker(s) as agents for the SELLER, prior to the expiration of such time, whereupon any payments made under this agreement shall be forthwith refunded and all other obligations of the parties hereto shall cease and this agreement shall be void without recourse to the parties hereto. For the purposes of this agreement, diligent efforts shall mean applying to one institutional mortgage lender currently making such loans and supplying all information requested by such lender.

16. INSURANCE

Until the delivery of the deed, the SELLER shall maintain insurance on said premises as follows:

Type of Insurance		Amount of Coverage
(a)	Fire	$ as presently insured
(b)	Extended coverage	$ as presently insured
(c)		

17. ASSIGNMENT OF INSURANCE

Unless otherwise notified in writing by the BUYER at least seven days before the time for delivery of the deed, and unless prevented from doing so by the refusal of the insurance company(s) involved to issue the same, the SELLER shall assign such insurance and deliver binders therefore in proper form to the BUYER at the time for performance of this agreement. In the event of refusal by the insurance company(s) to issue the same, the SELLER shall give notice thereof to the BUYER at least two business days before the time for performance of this agreement.

18. ADJUSTMENTS

Water and sewer use charges, operating expenses (if any) according to the schedule attached hereto or set forth below, and taxes for the then current year, shall be apportioned and full value shall be adjusted, as of the day of performance of this agreement and the net amount thereof shall be added to or deducted from, as the case may be, the purchase price payable by the BUYER at the time of delivery of the deed.

19. ADJUSTMENT OF UNASSESSED AND ABATED TAXES

If the amount of said taxes is not known at the time of the delivery of the deed, they shall be apportioned on the basis of the taxes assessed for the preceding year, with a reapportionment as soon as the new tax rate and valuation can be ascertained; and, if the taxes which are to be apportioned shall thereafter be reduced by abatement, the amount of such abatement, less the reasonable cost of obtaining the same shall be apportioned between the parties, provided that neither party shall be obligated to institute or prosecute proceedings for an abatement unless herein otherwise agreed.

20. BROKER'S FEE

A broker's fee for professional services of $11,500 is due from the SELLER to Ben Broker, LLC, the Broker(s) herein, but if the SELLER pursuant to the terms of clause 22 hereof retains the deposits made hereunder by the Buyer, said Broker(s) shall be entitled to receive from the SELLER an amount equal to one-half the amount so retained or an amount equal to the broker's fee for services according to this contract, whichever is the lesser.

21. BROKER(s) WARRANTY

The Broker(s) named herein warrant(s) that he (they) is (are) duly licensed as such by the Commonwealth of Massachusetts.

22. DEPOSIT

All deposits made hereunder shall be held in escrow by Ben Broker, LLC as agent for the SELLER, subject to the terms of this agreement an shall be duly accounted for at the time for performance of this agreement. If the deposit is in the form of a check, the associate acknowledges receipt of said deposit when the check clears the buyer's bank and has been paid.

23. BUYER'S DEFAULT; DAMAGES

If the BUYER shall fail to fulfill the BUYER'S agreements herein, all deposits made hereunder by the BUYER shall be retained by the SELLER as liquidated damages and this shall be the Seller's sole and exclusive remedy at law or in equity.

24. SALE OF PERSONAL PROPERTY **NOT APPLICABLE**

    NONE

The BUYER agrees to buy from the SELLER the articles of personal property enumerated on the attached list for the price of $ **NOT APPLICABLE** and the SELLER agrees to deliver to the BUYER upon delivery of the deed hereunder, a warranty bill of sale therefore on payment of said price. The provisions of this clause shall constitute an agreement separate and apart from the provisions herein contained with respect to the real estate, and any breach of the terms and conditions of this clause shall have no effect on the provisions of this agreement with respect to the real estate.

RELEASE BY HUSBAND OR WIFE

The SELLER'S spouse hereby agrees to join in said deed and to release and convey all statutory and other rights and interests in said premises.

26. BROKER AS PARTY **NOT APPLICABLE**

The broker(s) names herein, join(s) in this agreement and become(s) a party hereto, in so far as any provisions of this agreement expressly apply to him (them), and to any amendments or modifications of such provisions to which he (they) agree(s) in writing.

27 LIABILITY OF TRUSTEE, SHAREHOLDER, BENEFICIARY, etc.

If the SELLER or BUYER executes this agreement in a representative or fiduciary capacity, only the principal or the estate represented shall be bound, and neither the SELLER or BUYER so executing, nor any shareholder or beneficiary of any trust, shall be personally liable for any obligation, express or implied, hereunder.

28. WARRANTIES AND REPRESENTATIONS

The BUYER acknowledges that the BUYER has not been influenced to enter into this transaction nor has he relied upon any warranties or representations nor set forth or incorporated in this agreement or previously made in writing, except for the following additional warranties and representations, if any, made by either the SELLER or their Broker

    NONE

29. CONSTRUCTION OF AGREEMENT

This instrument, executed in triplicate is to be construed as a Massachusetts contract, to take effect as a sealed instrument, sets forth the entire contract between the parties, is binding upon and enures to the benefit of the parties hereto and their respective heirs, devises, executors, administrators, successors and assigns, and may be canceled, modified or amended only by a written instrument executed by both the SELLER and the BUYER. If two or more persons are named herein as BUYER their obligations hereunder shall be joint and several. The captions and notes are used only a matter of convenience and are not be considered a part of this agreement or to be used in determining the intent of the parties to it.

30. LEAD PAINT LAW

Because PROPERTY WAS CONSTRUCTED PRIOR TO 1978, PARTIES HAVE SIGNED LEAD PAINT "PROPERTY TRANSFER NOTIFICATION CERTIFICATION FORM"

31. ADDITIONAL PROVISIONS

The initialed riders, if any, attached hereto, are incorporated herein by reference.

32. SPECIAL CLAUSES:

Said purchase is subject to satisfactory Title V inspection to be provided to Buyer five (5) days prior to closing.

NOTICE: This is a legal document that creates binding obligations. If not understood, consult an attorney.

This Agreement signed this ____ day of _____, in the year _____.

SELLER: _____

BUYER: _____

BROKER: _____

EXHIBIT A3

Seller's Statement of Property Condition

For details, see: *8–Disclosure Issues* on page 28.

Seller's Statement of Property Condition

On this _____ day of _____, 20____, the "Seller(s)" listed below have completed this Statement of Condition concerning the real property and fixtures (the "Property") located at

_____.

This Statement is a disclosure of the condition of the Property to the best of the Seller's knowledge, but should not be construed as a substitute for a thorough inspection of the Property by a prospective buyer. If nothing is noted in any of the component sections listed below, Seller knows of nothing that would pose a problem affecting such component. (Separate sheets may be attached if noted below).

1. **House Systems and Structures**
   (electric wiring, central air cond.,
   plumbing, etcetera)

2. **Heating System**

3. **Insulation, Asbestos, Lead Paint**

4. **Land/Foundation**
   (earth instability, water/dampness in cellar)

5. **Roof** (leaks, repairs)

6. **Sewerage** (backup, drainage problems)

7. **Drainage/Water**
   (drainage, flooding problems)

8. **Electrical Systems** (changes, repairs)

9. **Neighborhood** (unusual noise)

10. **Radon Gas/ Mold**

11. **Other/General**

Seller:_____   Seller:_____

RECEIPT ACKNOWLEDGED on (date):_____

Buyer:_____   Buyer:_____

EXHIBIT A4

Closing Disclosure
(Seller/Buyer)

This five-page form is a statement of final loan terms and closing costs. The example that follows and others that are similar, are used by closing attorneys and escrow companies throughout the country. They are designed to capture literally everything the home seller and buyer (borrower) will pay for and receive in cash at the closing.

TIP For Home Sellers

There will be a number of costs to be adjusted (pro-rated) to the date of the closing, such as your mortgage interest and utility payments. In this regard, make absolutely sure to provide the closing attorney or escrow company these numbers and appropriate payment dates no later than three business days before the closing. Failure to do so could cost you time, money and aggravation.

For details, see: *10–Getting Ready for Your Closing* on page 30.

Closing Disclosure

This form is a statement of final loan terms and closing costs. Compare this document with your Loan Estimate.

Closing Information

Date Issued	4/15/2013
Closing Date	4/15/2013
Disbursement Date	4/15/2013
Settlement Agent	Epsilon Title Co.
File #	12-3456
Property	456 Somewhere Ave
	Anytown, ST 12345
Sale Price	$180,000

Transaction Information

Borrower	Michael Jones and Mary Stone
	123 Anywhere Street
	Anytown, ST 12345
Seller	Steve Cole and Amy Doe
	321 Somewhere Drive
	Anytown, ST 12345
Lender	Ficus Bank

Loan Information

Loan Term	30 years
Purpose	Purchase
Product	Fixed Rate
Loan Type	☒ Conventional ☐ FHA
	☐ VA ☐ _____
Loan ID #	123456789
MIC #	000654321

Loan Terms

		Can this amount increase after closing?
Loan Amount	$162,000	**NO**
Interest Rate	3.875%	**NO**
Monthly Principal & Interest *See Projected Payments below for your Estimated Total Monthly Payment*	$761.78	**NO**
		Does the loan have these features?
Prepayment Penalty		**YES** • **As high as $3,240** if you pay off the loan during the first 2 years
Balloon Payment		**NO**

Projected Payments

Payment Calculation	Years 1-7		Years 8-30	
Principal & Interest		$761.78		$761.78
Mortgage Insurance	+	82.35	+	—
Estimated Escrow *Amount can increase over time*	+	206.13	+	206.13
Estimated Total Monthly Payment		**$1,050.26**		**$967.91**

		This estimate includes	In escrow?
Estimated Taxes, Insurance & Assessments *Amount can increase over time* *See page 4 for details*	**$356.13** a month	☒ Property Taxes ☒ Homeowner's Insurance ☒ Other: Homeowner's Association Dues	YES YES NO

See Escrow Account on page 4 for details. You must pay for other property costs separately.

Costs at Closing

Closing Costs	$9,712.10	Includes $4,694.05 in Loan Costs + $5,018.05 in Other Costs – $0 in Lender Credits. *See page 2 for details.*
Cash to Close	$14,147.26	Includes Closing Costs. *See Calculating Cash to Close on page 3 for details.*

Closing Cost Details

Loan Costs		Borrower-Paid		Seller-Paid		Paid by Others
		At Closing	Before Closing	At Closing	Before Closing	
A. Origination Charges		**$1,802.00**				
01 0.25 % of Loan Amount (Points)		$405.00				
02 Application Fee		$300.00				
03 Underwriting Fee		$1,097.00				
04						
05						
06						
07						
08						
B. Services Borrower Did Not Shop For		**$236.55**				
01 Appraisal Fee	to John Smith Appraisers Inc.					$405.00
02 Credit Report Fee	to Information Inc.		$29.80			
03 Flood Determination Fee	to Info Co.	$20.00				
04 Flood Monitoring Fee	to Info Co.	$31.75				
05 Tax Monitoring Fee	to Info Co.	$75.00				
06 Tax Status Research Fee	to Info Co.	$80.00				
07						
08						
09						
10						
C. Services Borrower Did Shop For		**$2,655.50**				
01 Pest Inspection Fee	to Pests Co.	$120.50				
02 Survey Fee	to Surveys Co.	$85.00				
03 Title – Insurance Binder	to Epsilon Title Co.	$650.00				
04 Title – Lender's Title Insurance	to Epsilon Title Co.	$500.00				
05 Title – Settlement Agent Fee	to Epsilon Title Co.	$500.00				
06 Title – Title Search	to Epsilon Title Co.	$800.00				
07						
08						
D. TOTAL LOAN COSTS (Borrower-Paid)		**$4,694.05**				
Loan Costs Subtotals (A + B + C)		$4,664.25	$29.80			

Other Costs

		Borrower-Paid		Seller-Paid		Paid by Others
		At Closing	Before Closing	At Closing	Before Closing	
E. Taxes and Other Government Fees		**$85.00**				
01 Recording Fees	Deed: $40.00 Mortgage: $45.00	$85.00				
02 Transfer Tax	to Any State			$950.00		
F. Prepaids		**$2,120.80**				
01 Homeowner's Insurance Premium (12 mo.) to Insurance Co.		$1,209.96				
02 Mortgage Insurance Premium (mo.)						
03 Prepaid Interest ($17.44 per day from 4/15/13 to 5/1/13)		$279.04				
04 Property Taxes (6 mo.) to Any County USA		$631.80				
05						
G. Initial Escrow Payment at Closing		**$412.25**				
01 Homeowner's Insurance $100.83 per month for 2 mo.		$201.66				
02 Mortgage Insurance per month for mo.						
03 Property Taxes $105.30 per month for 2 mo.		$210.60				
04						
05						
06						
07						
08 Aggregate Adjustment		– 0.01				
H. Other		**$2,400.00**				
01 HOA Capital Contribution	to HOA Acre Inc.	$500.00				
02 HOA Processing Fee	to HOA Acre Inc.	$150.00				
03 Home Inspection Fee	to Engineers Inc.	$750.00			$750.00	
04 Home Warranty Fee	to XYZ Warranty Inc.			$450.00		
05 Real Estate Commission	to Alpha Real Estate Broker			$5,700.00		
06 Real Estate Commission	to Omega Real Estate Broker			$5,700.00		
07 Title – Owner's Title Insurance (optional) to Epsilon Title Co.		$1,000.00				
08						
I. TOTAL OTHER COSTS (Borrower-Paid)		**$5,018.05**				
Other Costs Subtotals (E + F + G + H)		$5,018.05				
J. TOTAL CLOSING COSTS (Borrower-Paid)		**$9,712.10**				
Closing Costs Subtotals (D + I)		$9,682.30	$29.80	$12,800.00	$750.00	$405.00
Lender Credits						

CLOSING DISCLOSURE

Calculating Cash to Close

Use this table to see what has changed from your Loan Estimate.

	Loan Estimate	Final	Did this change?
Total Closing Costs (J)	$8,054.00	$9,712.10	YES · See **Total Loan Costs (D)** and **Total Other Costs (I)**
Closing Costs Paid Before Closing	$0	– $29.80	YES · You paid these Closing Costs **before closing**
Closing Costs Financed (Paid from your Loan Amount)	$0	$0	NO
Down Payment/Funds from Borrower	$18,000.00	$18,000.00	NO
Deposit	– $10,000.00	– $10,000.00	NO
Funds for Borrower	$0	$0	NO
Seller Credits	$0	– $2,500.00	YES · See Seller Credits in **Section L**
Adjustments and Other Credits	$0	– $1,035.04	YES · See details in **Sections K and L**
Cash to Close	$16,054.00	$14,147.26	

Summaries of Transactions

Use this table to see a summary of your transaction.

BORROWER'S TRANSACTION

K. Due from Borrower at Closing	$189,762.30
01 Sale Price of Property	$180,000.00
02 Sale Price of Any Personal Property Included in Sale	
03 Closing Costs Paid at Closing (J)	$9,682.30
04	
Adjustments	
05	
06	
07	

Adjustments for Items Paid by Seller in Advance

08 City/Town Taxes to	
09 County Taxes to	
10 Assessments to	
11 HOA Dues 4/15/13 to 4/30/13	$80.00
12	
13	
14	
15	

L. Paid Already by or on Behalf of Borrower at Closing	$175,615.04
01 Deposit	$10,000.00
02 Loan Amount	$162,000.00
03 Existing Loan(s) Assumed or Taken Subject to	
04	
05 Seller Credit	$2,500.00
Other Credits	
06 Rebate from Epsilon Title Co.	$750.00
07	
Adjustments	
08	
09	
10	
11	

Adjustments for Items Unpaid by Seller

12 City/Town Taxes 1/1/13 to 4/14/13	$365.04
13 County Taxes to	
14 Assessments to	
15	
16	
17	

CALCULATION

Total Due from Borrower at Closing (K)	$189,762.30
Total Paid Already by or on Behalf of Borrower at Closing (L)	– $175,615.04
Cash to Close ☒ From ☐ To Borrower	**$14,147.26**

SELLER'S TRANSACTION

M. Due to Seller at Closing	$180,080.00
01 Sale Price of Property	$180,000.00
02 Sale Price of Any Personal Property Included in Sale	
03	
04	
05	
06	
07	
08	

Adjustments for Items Paid by Seller in Advance

09 City/Town Taxes to	
10 County Taxes to	
11 Assessments to	
12 HOA Dues 4/15/13 to 4/30/13	$80.00
13	
14	
15	
16	

N. Due from Seller at Closing	$115,665.04
01 Excess Deposit	
02 Closing Costs Paid at Closing (J)	$12,800.00
03 Existing Loan(s) Assumed or Taken Subject to	
04 Payoff of First Mortgage Loan	$100,000.00
05 Payoff of Second Mortgage Loan	
06	
07	
08 Seller Credit	$2,500.00
09	
10	
11	
12	
13	

Adjustments for Items Unpaid by Seller

14 City/Town Taxes 1/1/13 to 4/14/13	$365.04
15 County Taxes to	
16 Assessments to	
17	
18	
19	

CALCULATION

Total Due to Seller at Closing (M)	$180,080.00
Total Due from Seller at Closing (N)	– $115,665.04
Cash ☐ From ☒ To Seller	**$64,414.96**

Additional Information About This Loan

Loan Disclosures

Assumption
If you sell or transfer this property to another person, your lender
☐ will allow, under certain conditions, this person to assume this loan on the original terms.
☒ will not allow assumption of this loan on the original terms.

Demand Feature
Your loan
☐ has a demand feature, which permits your lender to require early repayment of the loan. You should review your note for details.
☒ does not have a demand feature.

Late Payment
If your payment is more than 15 days late, your lender will charge a late fee of 5% of the monthly principal and interest payment.

Negative Amortization (Increase in Loan Amount)
Under your loan terms, you
☐ are scheduled to make monthly payments that do not pay all of the interest due that month. As a result, your loan amount will increase (negatively amortize), and your loan amount will likely become larger than your original loan amount. Increases in your loan amount lower the equity you have in this property.
☐ may have monthly payments that do not pay all of the interest due that month. If you do, your loan amount will increase (negatively amortize), and, as a result, your loan amount may become larger than your original loan amount. Increases in your loan amount lower the equity you have in this property.
☒ do not have a negative amortization feature.

Partial Payments
Your lender
☒ may accept payments that are less than the full amount due (partial payments) and apply them to your loan.
☐ may hold them in a separate account until you pay the rest of the payment, and then apply the full payment to your loan.
☐ does not accept any partial payments.
If this loan is sold, your new lender may have a different policy.

Security Interest
You are granting a security interest in
456 Somewhere Ave., Anytown, ST 12345

You may lose this property if you do not make your payments or satisfy other obligations for this loan.

Escrow Account
For now, your loan
☒ will have an escrow account (also called an "impound" or "trust" account) to pay the property costs listed below. Without an escrow account, you would pay them directly, possibly in one or two large payments a year. Your lender may be liable for penalties and interest for failing to make a payment.

Escrow		
Escrowed Property Costs over Year 1	$2,473.56	Estimated total amount over year 1 for your escrowed property costs: *Homeowner's Insurance Property Taxes*
Non-Escrowed Property Costs over Year 1	$1,800.00	Estimated total amount over year 1 for your non-escrowed property costs: *Homeowner's Association Dues* You may have other property costs.
Initial Escrow Payment	$412.25	A cushion for the escrow account you pay at closing. See Section G on page 2.
Monthly Escrow Payment	$206.13	The amount included in your total monthly payment.

☐ will not have an escrow account because ☐ you declined it ☐ your lender does not offer one. You must directly pay your property costs, such as taxes and homeowner's insurance. Contact your lender to ask if your loan can have an escrow account.

No Escrow		
Estimated Property Costs over Year 1		Estimated total amount over year 1. You must pay these costs directly, possibly in one or two large payments a year.
Escrow Waiver Fee		

In the future,
Your property costs may change and, as a result, your escrow payment may change. You may be able to cancel your escrow account, but if you do, you must pay your property costs directly. If you fail to pay your property taxes, your state or local government may (1) impose fines and penalties or (2) place a tax lien on this property. If you fail to pay any of your property costs, your lender may (1) add the amounts to your loan balance, (2) add an escrow account to your loan, or (3) require you to pay for property insurance that the lender buys on your behalf, which likely would cost more and provide fewer benefits than what you could buy on your own.

Loan Calculations

Total of Payments. Total you will have paid after you make all payments of principal, interest, mortgage insurance, and loan costs, as scheduled. — $285,803.36

Finance Charge. The dollar amount the loan will cost you. — $118,830.27

Amount Financed. The loan amount available after paying your upfront finance charge. — $162,000.00

Annual Percentage Rate (APR). Your costs over the loan term expressed as a rate. This is not your interest rate. — 4.174%

Total Interest Percentage (TIP). The total amount of interest that you will pay over the loan term as a percentage of your loan amount. — 69.46%

Questions? If you have questions about the loan terms or costs on this form, use the contact information below. To get more information or make a complaint, contact the Consumer Financial Protection Bureau at **www.consumerfinance.gov/mortgage-closing**

Other Disclosures

Appraisal
If the property was appraised for your loan, your lender is required to give you a copy at no additional cost at least 3 days before closing. If you have not yet received it, please contact your lender at the information listed below.

Contract Details
See your note and security instrument for information about
 • what happens if you fail to make your payments,
 • what is a default on the loan,
 • situations in which your lender can require early repayment of the loan, and
 • the rules for making payments before they are due.

Liability after Foreclosure
If your lender forecloses on this property and the foreclosure does not cover the amount of unpaid balance on this loan,
☒ state law may protect you from liability for the unpaid balance. If you refinance or take on any additional debt on this property, you may lose this protection and have to pay any debt remaining even after foreclosure. You may want to consult a lawyer for more information.
☐ state law does not protect you from liability for the unpaid balance.

Refinance
Refinancing this loan will depend on your future financial situation, the property value, and market conditions. You may not be able to refinance this loan.

Tax Deductions
If you borrow more than this property is worth, the interest on the loan amount above this property's fair market value is not deductible from your federal income taxes. You should consult a tax advisor for more information.

Contact Information

	Lender	Mortgage Broker	Real Estate Broker (B)	Real Estate Broker (S)	Settlement Agent
Name	Ficus Bank		Omega Real Estate Broker Inc.	Alpha Real Estate Broker Co.	Epsilon Title Co.
Address	4321 Random Blvd. Somecity, ST 12340		789 Local Lane Sometown, ST 12345	987 Suburb Ct. Someplace, ST 12340	123 Commerce Pl. Somecity, ST 12344
NMLS ID					
ST License ID			Z765416	Z61456	Z61616
Contact	Joe Smith		Samuel Green	Joseph Cain	Sarah Arnold
Contact NMLS ID	12345				
Contact ST License ID			P16415	P51461	PT1234
Email	joesmith@ficusbank.com		sam@omegare.biz	joe@alphare.biz	sarah@epsilontitle.com
Phone	123-456-7890		123-555-1717	321-555-7171	987-555-4321

Confirm Receipt

By signing, you are only confirming that you have received this form. You do not have to accept this loan because you have signed or received this form.

_____   _____   _____   _____
Applicant Signature   Date   Co-Applicant Signature   Date

CLOSING DISCLOSURE

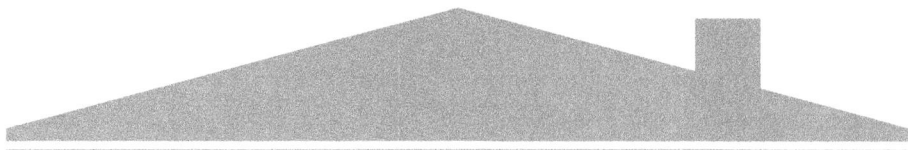

EXHIBIT A5

Before and After Moving Checklists

Before Moving Check List

This list covers all the things you should take care of before you move out.

Moving Into Your New Home Check List

This list identifies all the new services and contacts you need to establish in your new community.

Before Moving Check List

☐ **Change of address**

☐ Present post office	☐ Friends, relatives	☐ Future post office
☐ Insurance companies	☐ Associations	☐ Magazines
☐ Banks	☐ Registry of Motor Vehicles	☐ Book clubs
☐ Religious groups	☐ Catalogue companies	☐ Social Security
☐ Charge cards	☐ State and local agencies	☐ Department stores

☐ **Utilities** – arrange for final billing:

☐ Electric   ☐ Water   ☐ Gas   ☐ Telephone

☐ **Cancel all home deliveries**

☐ **Obtain school transcripts**

☐ **Additional insurance**
Check with your agent on coverage of household goods en route to your new home

☐ **Family professionals** – Inform your . . .

☐ Doctors   ☐ Dentist   ☐ Attorney   ☐ Veterinarian

☐ Refill drug prescriptions

☐ Obtain copies of all pertinent records

☐ **Birth and/or baptism certificate**

☐ **Closing papers**
Leave the necessary closing papers with your attorney or Realtor (on your present home).

☐ **Moving company**
Contact and schedule your moving date

☐ **Pets**
Arrange transportation of your pets

☐ **Inventory**
Take complete inventory

☐ **House keys**
Leave your keys with appropriate individual
☐ New owner   ☐ Realtor   ☐ Attorney

Moving Into Your New Home Check List

☐ **Utilities** (Be sure your utilities are transferred into your name and turned on)

    ☐ Electric   ☐ Water   ☐ Gas   ☐ Telephone

☐ **Post office**
Request deliveries

☐ **School**
Register children

☐ **Auto registration**
Driver's license
Insurance

☐ **Banks**
Establish new accounts

☐ **Family professionals** – establish new:

    ☐ Doctors   ☐ Dentist   ☐ Attorney   ☐ Veterinarian

☐ **Inventory** – take complete inventory

☐ **Extracurricular / summer activities registration**

☐ **Voter registration**

☐ **Sports facilities**

☐ **Organizations**

☐ **Trash disposal facility / removal service**

☐ **Library card**

☐ **Pool / beach registration**

☐ **Emergency telephone numbers:**

Doctor: _____   **Police:** _____

Fire: _____   **Poison Info Center:** _____

Ambulance: _____   **Veterinarian:** _____

Other: _____   **Other:** _____

EXHIBIT B1

Offer to Purchase Form

Essentially, this form sets the foundation for the P&S Agreement—if the offer is accepted by the seller.

Note the *Duration of Offer*. This may vary depending on the buyers' strategy. In this example, the buyers and their agent have decided to put some timing pressure on the seller and the closing. Failure to do so could cost you time, money and aggravation.

For more background, see: *14–Making an Offer,* on page 40.

Offer To Purchase Real Estate   <u>EXAMPLE</u>

THIS 4th DAY OF _____ October_____, 20 09____ ("Offer Date").

Barry R. and Beverly Buyer_____("Buyer"), presently residing at

100 Circuit Street, Holbrook, MA 02117_____,
HEREWITH MAKES AN OFFER TO PURCHASE the property of

Samuel and Sarah Seller_____("Seller"), located at

11 Willow Lane, Norwell, MA 02061_____("Property").

TERMS OF OFFER ("Offer")

1.   **Purchase Price:** $ 445,000___

2.   **Payable:** $ ___3,000_____ deposit herewith made out to and held by _Seller_____ ;
     $ _19,000_____ upon signing a Purchase and Sale Agreement ("P&S") satisfactory to both Seller and Buyer; and
     $ 423,000_____ to be paid at the time of delivery of the deed.

3   **Duration of Offer:** this Offer is good until 9:00 PM on October 5_____ 2009__ ("expiration").

          If acceptable, Seller shall execute this Offer and return a copy to Buyer on or before expiration.
          If not acceptable, Seller shall return the deposit to the Buyer immediately following expiration.

4.   **Buyer Representation** (initial one):

     (initials) Buyer HAS NOT been introduced to and/or shown the Property by any real estate agent/broker.

     _____ Buyer HAS been introduced to and/or shown the Property by the following real estate agent/broker:

          _____

5.   **Purchase and Sale Agreement ("P&S Agreement")**

     Parties agree that if and when this Offer is accepted by Seller ("Acceptance Date"), then no later than seven days from said Acceptance Date they will execute a Standard Form P&S Agreement (or any format substantially similar thereto) containing the essential terms contained herein and further subject to the following:

     a.   Buyer will complete all desired and/or required Property Inspections to Buyer's satisfaction no later than 14 _ days from the date the P&S Agreement is fully executed;

     b.   Buyer will secure a firm mortgage commitment from a mortgage lender not in excess of $ 350,000___ at prevailing rates and terms no later than midnight on November 5, 2009_____;

     c.   Title will transfer from Seller to Buyer at the applicable Registry of Deeds on December 14, 2009_____.

6.   **Additional Provisions**

     a.   If dwelling on Property was constructed prior to 1978, a "Property Transfer Notification Certification" must be signed by the parties before execution of the P&S Agreement.

This is a legal document that creates binding obligations. If not understood, consult an attorney.

WITNESS my/our hand(s) and seal(s) on the date first set forth above.

Buyer:___(Signature) _____   Buyer:___(Signature) _____

OFFER ACCEPTED at _____ (AM) (PM) on _____, 20_____ (Acceptance Date).

Seller:_____   Seller:_____

EXHIBIT B2

Home Inspection Report

The attached example shows just the title page of this lengthy, detailed report. The balance of this report covered:

- Garage and Basement
- Central Heating and Cooling
- Electrical System
- Plumbing System
- Kitchen
- Appliances
- Interior
- Attic Ventilation/Insulation

For more background, see: *15–The Home Inspection*, on page 42.

PROPERTY INSPECTION REPORT

1

XYZ
*Property Inspection
Company*

Our rating system is as follows:
A: Indicates item is functioning as originally intended.
B: This item is functioning less than originally intended. Maintenance, repair or upgrade is suggested.
C: Caution is advised with this item, as it is not functioning.
NR: Not inspected. No rating.
△: Further consultation with a contractor is advised.

EXTERIOR

	A	B	C	NR	△
1. Roof type Pitch	☑	☑	☐	☐	☐
Surface type asphalt	☐	☑	☐	☑	☑
How viewed Binoculars					
2. Exterior of Chimney: See Comment E	☑	☑	☐	☐	☐
(Flue Liner not included)					
type Brick clean out					
cricket flashing sealer X					
3. Exterior siding: Type Vinyl/wood	☐	☑	☐	☐	☐
4. Exterior trim: Type wood	☐	☑	☐	☐	☐
5. Exposed gutters and downspouts:					
Type Aluminum/Vinyl	☐	☑	☐	☐	☐
6. Perimeter drainage and grading	☐	☑	☐	☐	☐
7. Basement windows	☑	☐	☐	☐	☐
8. Window wells	☐	☐	☐	☑	☐
9. Exterior faucet	☑	☐	☐	☐	☐
10. Electric service entry	☐	☑	☐	☐	☐
☑ weather head/drip loop ☑ meter					
☐ underground ☑ service amperage 100					
11. Exterior outlets	☐	☑	☑	☐	☑
12. Exterior lighting/Oil fill pipe	☑	☐	☐	☐	☐
13. Walkways Type Cement	☑	☐	☐	☐	☐
14. Driveway Type Asphalt	☑	☐	☐	☐	☐
15. Attached decks/porches/stairs					
☑ front Type cement	☐	☑	☐	☐	☐
☑ rear Type wood - to bench	☐	☑	☐	☐	☐
☐ side Type wood deck	☐	☑	☐	☐	☐
16. Patios Type Cement	☑	☐	☐	☐	☐
17. Retaining Walls within 10ft of structure	☑	☐	☐	☐	☐

Handwritten notes:
(1) See Note A,B,C,J - design of shed dormers prevent
(2) Visual access - Consult owner or contractor for condition - roof shows signs of aging in some places - expect repairs or replacement
(3) See Comment E - flashing sealer is a temporary fix and should be checked annually
(3a) Scrape, prime, recaulk paint as needed - remove, investigate repair as needed any soft or rotted wood
(5) See Comment D - extend downspouts away from house to prevent water penetration
(6) Trim trees and bushes away from house to avoid water and insect intrusion - Grade soil away from foundation to prevent water ponding - minimize earth to wood contact - See note K
(9) See Comment G
(10) Maintain watertight seal around entry cable into meter box and house
(11) Exterior outlet facing ocean is not working - Consult owner or contractor for necessary repairs or upgrades
(12) See Note H
(15) Seal cracks with hydraulic cement as needed - Add handrails to bench stairs for safety - Recommend adding cross bracing to deck stairs for added strength - height of railing around rear deck appears to be low - repair as needed - See Comment I - No access under rear deck

IMPORTANT INFORMATION PLEASE READ:
A. Manufacturers of asphalt shingles, on average, provide a twenty year warranty. This should not be confused with the actual roof life. Actual roof life cannot be predicted due to many variables. B. It is advised that reserves be set aside for repairs or eventual replacement. It is suggested that no more than two layers of roofing lie on roof. C. Check flashing yearly. D. To prevent water damage to roof, sheathing, walls, ceilings and structural members, gutters and down spouts must be kept clean and clear and free of debris. It is suggested that you check periodically to ensure all is working well. E. Local regulations in some communities require the presence of a flue liner when using certain fuels. Consult your local authorities. F. Window wells should be cleaned annually. G. Exterior faucets should be drained during the colder months to prevent freezing. H. Driveway should be sealed to extend its life. I. The underside of decks and porches not accessible at the time of this inspection should be made accessible to check for damage, rot or infestation. J. You should verify the roof's age through the broker, owner, or contractor. Also see page 8, Comment D. K. Wood contacting the ground is conducive to wood-destroying activity. Therefore it should be removed or maintained.

EXHIBIT B3

Mortgage Pre-Approval Letter

For background and details of when and how to seek and use a pre-approval letter, see: *13–Getting Started Right,* on page 36.

XYZ
Mortgage Services

September 19, 2013

Mr. John Smith
Mrs. Lisa Smith
400 Jerome Street
Berkley, MA 02779

Dear Mr. & Mrs. Smith:

This letter is intended to confirm your pre-approval for a 30 year fixed rate FHA mortgage based on a purchase price of $360,000.00.

This pre-approval is based on our review of your current income, employment history, credit, and available assets.

This pre-approval is subject to a satisfactory purchase and sales agreement, appraisal, title examination, and final investor approval.

If you or your real estate broker has any questions, please feel free to contact me at (781) 525-5555.

Sincerely,

Joe Originator
Senior Loan Officer

EXHIBIT C1

Rental Value Analysis Format

Although this form was developed for estimating the rental value of homes for rent, it can also apply to apartments. Note that the general approach to estimating the rental value is the same as that found in the *Home Appraisal Format* contained In *Exhibit A1* on page 89.

This Rental Value Analysis has been designed for use by a rental and/or property management professional to complete on behalf of the homeowner.

RENTAL VALUE ANALYSIS

Relocation
Resources
Inc.

Owner(s): _____ Date of Inspection: _____

Subject Property Address: Street and Number _____

Town or City _____

County _____ State _____ Zip _____

MARKET DATA APPROACH TO VALUE   *(Mark "+" or "–" on Specific Comp Data, If Applicable)*

DATA	SUBJECT	COMP 1	COMP 2
Address:			
Date of Lease			
Days on Market			
Original (Asking) Rental Price			
Final (Actual) Rental Price			
Distance From Subject			
Location (Tops, Average, et cetera)			
Lot Size			
Real Estate Taxes			
Special Assessments			
Architectural Style			
Age/Condition (Excellent, Good, et cetera)			
Square Feet (Gross Living Area)			
Number of Rooms			
Number of Bedrooms			
Number of Baths			
Number of Fireplaces			
Basement (Full, Partial, Crawl, Slab)			
Garage (# & Att, Det, Under)			
Central Air (Yes or No)			
Special Features			

OPINION OF FAIR RENTAL VALUE

I estimate that the Fair Rental Value* of the Subject Property, as of the Date of Inspection, is between $_____ and $_____ /Month, which includes tenant's use of fixtures, appliances (□ and personal property) with tenant paying, in addition to rent, all required utilities and services. I further estimate it will take _____ to _____ days to find a credit-worthy, responsible tenant to lease at this figure. In my opinion, special advertising □ is □ is not required to achieve the projected marketing time frame. I certify that to the best of my knowledge, the statements made in this report are true; that no significant information has knowingly been withheld; that I have personally inspected the Subject Property, both inside and out; that I have no interest (present or contemplated) in the Subject Property; that all contingent and limiting conditions are stated herein.

SIGNATURE: _____ NAME (Print) _____

FIRM _____ DATE _____

* "Fair Rental Value" - The highest rental price which the Subject Property will bring (in its present condititon) if exposed for lease on the open market, allowing a reasonable time to find a credit-worthy, responsible tenant who leases with the knowledge of all the uses for which it may be properly used.

Page 1 of 2   2RRL-R2

RENTAL VALUE ANALYSIS

• REFURBISHING / REPAIRS

In your opinion does Subject Property require refurbishing or repairs (interior and/or exterior) prior to marketing? ☐ Yes ☐ No

If "Yes" - Describe   ESTIMATE OF COST

$_____

$_____

$_____

$_____

If Refurbished/Repaired as specified . . .

Rental Value would increase to $_____ / month; Marketing Time ☐ would not decrease ☐ would decrease to _____ days.

• RATE THE FOLLOWING	CONDITION	• ANY EVIDENCE OF FOLLOWING? (If so, please describe)
Quality of Construction (Materials and Finish)		☐ Water Dampness
Overall Condition of Improvements		☐ Termites/Pests
Floor Plan and Traffic Pattern		☐ Well Problems
Closets and Storage · Adequacy		☐ Roof Problems
Insulation · Adequacy		☐ Floor Buckling
Plumbing · Adequacy and Condition		☐ Settlement Cracks
Electrical · Adequacy and Condition		☐ Dry Rot
Heating/Air Cond. · Adequacy and Condition		☐ Septic/Cesspool Problems
Comments (on factors that add to or detract from value of property):		☐ Cracked Slab
		☐ Soil Problem (erosion/drainage)
		☐ Foundation Cracks
		☐ Poor Water Pressure
		☐ Other

In your opinion, are any professional inspections required prior to offering this property for lease?   Yes ☐   No ☐

If "Yes," which inspection(s) would you recommend? (list) _____

• NEIGHBORHOOD and SITE

Neighborhood Character: ☐ Urban ☐ Suburban ☐ Rural. Built-up_____%. Values: ☐ Increasing ☐ Stable ☐ Declining

Use: Single Family _____%   2-4 Family _____%   Apartments _____% Condos/Co-ops _____ % Commercial _____%.

Price Range of Homes: $_____ (low) to $_____ (high) Predominant Value: $_____

Age Range of Homes: _____ years (oldest) to_____ years (newest). Predominant Age:_____ years.

General Appearance of Homes in Area:_____

Is Subject Property located in area known for potential hazards (such as, flood, fire, slide, et cetera)? ☐ Yes ☐ No

If "Yes" please explain: _____

Street: ☐ Public ☐ Private ☐ Paved ☐ Dirt ☐ Storm Drains ☐ Sidewalks ☐ Curbs ☐ Street Lights

Public: ☐ Electricity   ☐ Gas   ☐ Water   ☐ Sewerage

How many homes in neighborhood for rent now? # _____ Rented now # _____ Lowest Rent $_____ Highest Rent $_____

• SUPPLY and DEMAND

Which one of the following best describes the present single family Rental Market?

☐ Tenant's Market
More rentals than possible tenants

☐ Balanced Market
Supply/Demand about the same

☐ Landlords' Market
More possible tenants than rentals.

• BROKER'S GENERAL COMMENTS:

AFFIX PHOTO HERE

Street-front angle giving perspective of how dwelling is located on lot.

Page 2 of 2

EXHIBIT C2

Rental Application Format

Note the factual questions on page 1 and the *Applicant's* Understanding on page 2.

It is extremely important to get the applicant's authorization to verify the answers to ALL the factual questions, particularly those pertaining to prior landlords and employers.

| | **RENTAL APPLICATION** | Relocation Resources Inc. |

PREMISES

Application is herewith made to lease premises at _____
Desired length of Lease: _____ Months. Beginning (Date): _____ Ending (Date):_____
Use of Premises (Write name, age, and relationship of all occupants and, if appropriate, describe pets):
_____

APPLICANT	**CO-APPLICANT**
Name: _____	Name: _____
Age: _____ Social Security #: _____	Age: _____ Social Security #: _____
Present Address: _____	_____ Telephone #: _____

APPLICANT'S EMPLOYER	**CO- APPLICANT'S EMPLOYER**
Company: _____	Company: _____
How Long Employed? ____ Years. Annual Salary: $ _____	How Long Employed? ____ Years. Annual Salary: $ _____
Your Title/Position: _____	Your Title/Position: _____
To whom should we talk regarding your employment?	To whom should we talk regarding your employment?
Name: _____	Name: _____
Title: _____	Title: _____
Telephone: _____	Telephone: _____

APPLICANT'S PRIOR EMPLOYER	**CO-APPLICANT'S PRIOR EMPLOYER**
Company: _____	Company: _____
How Long Employed? ____ Years. Annual Salary: $ _____	How Long Employed? ____ Years. Annual Salary: $ _____
Your Title/Position: _____	Your Title/Position: _____
Who should we talk to regarding your employment?	Who should we talk to regarding your employment?
Name: _____	Name: _____
Title: _____	Title: _____
Telephone: _____	Telephone: _____

PRESENT and PAST HOUSING

How long at present address? _____ Monthly Rental: $ _____ Utilities paid for: $ _____

Landlord's Name: _____ Telephone: _____

Last Previous Address: _____

How long at previous address? _____ Monthly Rental: $ _____ Utilities paid for: $ _____

Landlord's Name: _____ Telephone: _____

ADDITIONAL INFORMATION

Are there, or have there ever been, any judgments, law suits, or bill collection proceedings against you?	☐ Yes	☐ No
Are you now, or have you ever been, a defendant in any suit or legal action?	☐ Yes	☐ No
Have you ever been foreclosed on or declareld or taken personal or business bankruptcy?	☐ Yes	☐ No
Have you ever been sued or evicted for non-payment of rent or otherwise?	☐ Yes	☐ No

    Page 1 of 2 (Over)   RRL-R10

APPLICANT'S UNDERSTANDING

I understand that any and all of the information provided by me herein may be used by the Landlord or the Landlord's Agent to determine my reputation for meeting my financial obligations and respect for other people's property. I freely give my consent to the Landlord and/or the Landlord's Agent to consult with any of the persons or institutions named or not named who may have knowledge of my financial reliability and respect for other people's property.

I understand that this Rental Application does not constitute a commitment to lease and that a written Lease Agreement will be prepared if my application is approved. I further understand that the Lease Agreement must be signed by both the Landlord (or the Landlord's Agent) and me in order to be valid. I understand that the Lease Agreement is a legally binding contract and I have been informed that I should seek legal advise prior to executing the Lease Agreement.

I herewith pay the non-refundable sum of $ _____ for a consumer credit check/application fee with the clear understanding that this Application is subject to approval and acceptance. If this Application is not approved and accepted, I understand that there will be no refund of said consumer credit check/ application fee, and I hereby waive any claim for damages by reason of non-approval and/or non-acceptance of this Application.

If this Application is approved and accepted, and I execute the Lease Agreement, I understand that I will have to pay: (1) the first monthly installment of rent in advance; and, (2) the security deposit within ten (10) days after being notified of acceptance, and before possession is given. I understand that I will apply for all utilities and services to the leased premises before taking occupancy and will pay deposits therefore if required.

CREDIT REPORTS

I understand that a consumer credit report may be requested from one or more consumer reporting agencies (credit bureaus) in connection with this application. Subsequent consumer credit reports may be requested or used in connection with any update, renewal or extension of the lease requested by this Application. If I request, I understand that I will be informed whether any consumer credit report was requested and, if so, the name and address of the consumer reporting agency which furnished the report. The Landlord or his Agent may request and use the consumer credit report, and they, or anyone they may ask or anyone who so requests, may exchange credit information about me in connection with this application or any lease created as a result of this application.

I understand that the truth of the information contained herein is essential, and if the Landlord or his Agent determines that any answer or statement contained herein is false or misleading, any lease granted in reliance of the truth of this Application may be cancelled at the option of the Landlord or his Agent. This Application shall become part of any Lease Agreement executed between the Landlord and myself, and any false or misleading statement shall be considered a breach of said Lease Agreement and the Landlord or his Agent shall have the option to cancel the lease granted by virtue of this application.

I hereby affirm that my answers to the foregoing questions are true and correct, and that I have not knowingly withheld any fact or circumstance which would, if disclosed, affect my Application unfavorably.

I understand that if more than one party signs as Applicants herewith, the words "I," "My," and "Me" as used herein apply to all parties and the understanding of the Applicants herein shall be the joint and several obligation of each party.

_____   _____
Applicant's Signature   Applicant's Signature

Date: _____

Page 2 of 2

ACKNOWLEDGMENTS

Over the years, there are so many people I'm indebted to for sharing their real estate expertise and opinions with me. They number in the thousands.

The following people exemplify this great group of professionals:

John & Betty Boebinger – Canton, Ohio

Dick Christopher – Wilmington, Delaware

Dave Cole – Vail, Colorado

Alfred Edge – Galveston, Texas

John Gallinger – Syracuse, New York

Ebby Halliday – Dallas, Texas

Joe Klock – Philadelphia, Pennsylvania

Bill & Steve Lauderback – Kansas City & Wichita, Kansas

Jay Levine – Los Angeles, California

Hannalore McCuen – Paris, France

Bill Moore – Denver, Colorado

Mona Radwan – Cairo, Egypt

Steve Murray – Castle Rock, Colorado

Chip Roach – Philadelphia, Pennsylvania

Loren Schulenberg, 3M – Saint Paul, Minnesota

Frank & Kevin Sheehan – Melbourne, Australia

Beverly Sunn – Hong Kong, China

Jim Weichert – Chatham, New Jersey

When I founded Relocation Resources International (RRI), for the first time in my career I needed substantial lines of credit to buy, hold and resell thousands of homes of transferred employees—and

I was starting from scratch with little capital and track record in the industry. If it hadn't been for Jim Clark of Chase Manhattan Bank, a caring, knowledgeable banker having faith in me at a truly critical time, I don't know if RRI would have become the great success it eventually became.

As always, I'm most indebted to my wife, partner and best friend. Besides being a great wife, mother and grandmother, Judy has been my leading critic, editor and proof reader for the five published books I've written.

Lastly, special thanks to Tom Benoit, Chuck Cherry, Laura Glinski, Matt Melvin and Brian Molisse for their very helpful critical reviews.

INDEX